KV-513-093

A Quantitative Approach to Software Management

The ami handbook

Kevin Pulford
GEC–Marconi Software Systems

Annie Kuntzmann-Combelles
Objectif Technologie

Stephen Shirlaw
GEC–Alsthom

ADDISON-WESLEY PUBLISHING COMPANY
Wokingham, England • Reading, Massachusetts • Menlo Park, California
New York • Don Mills, Ontario • Amsterdam • Bonn • Sydney • Singapore
Tokyo • Madrid • San Juan • Milan • Paris • Mexico City • Seoul • Taipei

© 1996 Addison-Wesley Publishers Ltd.
© 1996 Addison-Wesley Publishing Company Inc.

All rights reserved. No part of this publication may be reproduced, stored in a retrieval system, or transmitted in any form or by any means, electronic, mechanical, photocopying, recording or otherwise, without prior written permission of the publisher.

Many of the designations used by manufacturers and sellers to distinguish their products are claimed as trademarks. Addison-Wesley has made every attempt to supply trademark information about manufacturers and their products mentioned in this book. A list of the trademark designations and their owners appears below.

Cover designed by op den Brouw, Design & Illustration, Reading
and printed by The Riverside Printing Co. (Reading) Ltd
Text design by Carla Turchini
Typeset by Express Graphics Ltd, Cliddesden, Basingstoke
Printed and bound by Biddles of Guildford
First printed 1995

ISBN 0–201–87746–5

British Library Cataloguing-in-Publication Data
A catalogue record for this book is available from the British Library.

Library of Congress Cataloging-in-Publication Data applied for

Trademark Notice
EXCEL™ is a trademark of Microsoft Corporation
1–2–3™ is a trademark of Lotus Development Corporation
Trademarks for the term **ami** and the nautilus logo have been applied for by the **ami** User Group

A Quantitative Approach
to Software Management

Preface

Why **ami**?

At the beginning of 1991 a consortium of European companies started a three year project aimed at improving the uptake and exploitation of measurement techniques within the software community. This was the start of the **ami** project (application of metrics in industry). The approach used by the project was to make the technology and techniques of metrics and measurement available in a simple, straightforward and understandable form that could be easily implemented. The result was the **ami** handbook and the **ami** method. This book is an updated version of the original **ami** handbook and reflects the experience of applying the **ami** method following the completion of the **ami** project.

It is now widely accepted that the use of measurement gives the following benefits:

- improved project planning and management of projects

- alignment of software development to business objectives

- cost-effective improvement programmes

- improved project communication

This book is for managers and engineers who need to apply quantitative techniques to improve the understanding and management of their software projects. The **ami** approach is designed for those who have yet to start on software measurement. It will also aid managers who have already started, and want to optimize the benefits from their measurement effort. **ami**'s flexible approach, complementing mature management practices, fulfils the varied and complex decision-making needs of the software industry.

Software is a strategic component in business and industry. Despite the coming of age of the software engineering industry, there are still many difficulties in producing good quality software within budget and on time. The increasing availability of methods and tools and the cost of investing in them makes it essential to evaluate new options continuously and to improve current practices. This book addresses this issue with a method for measurement to support the control and improvement of the software development process. It is a clear guide showing you how to:

- assess your environment

- define goals for measurement

- implement a measurement plan

- exploit collected data

The **ami** book

Fast track sections are provided at the start of Chapters 3 to 6 for those who require an overview of the **ami** method.

The first chapter gives an overview of software measurement and the **ami** approach for those wanting a grounding in the use of quantitative approaches. The second chapter presents the **ami** method and how it is used. It addresses managers and others who need to understand the main features of the method.

The method is developed in the subsequent four chapters. The bodies of the chapters contain a complete description of how to apply each step of the method. Other sections of the book give further support: Chapter 7 gives references for further reading; Appendix 1 presents the SEI Software Capability Maturity Model; Appendix 2 provides examples of goals and metrics; and Appendix 3 gives definitions of the most relevant measurements which you can apply. Appendix 4 gives three further case studies of the application of the **ami** method. Appendix 4 is followed by a complete glossary of keywords used in the book.

For most of the steps we have given a list of recommendations to help you apply the method and avoid some of the pitfalls. A continuous example has been provided to show the application of **ami** to a project and to demonstrate in detail how **ami** is applied in practice.

Acknowledgements

The **ami** project was sponsored by DGXIII of the Commission of the European Communities through the ESPRIT programme. The project was specifically funded by ESPRIT to develop a practical approach backed by full-scale tests on software projects. The ami consortium has developed the **ami** method firmly grounded on common sense and well-tried practice.

The consortium consisted of the following European organizations:

Alcatel–ELIN (Austria)

Bull AG (Germany)

GEC–Alsthom (France)

GEC–Marconi Software Systems (UK)

RWTÜV Rheinish-Westfalischer Technisher Uberwachungs-Verein (Germany)

Objectif Technologie (formally Corelis Technologie) (France)

O.Group (Italy)

TECHNOS (Grupo SGS CIAT) (Spain)

South Bank University (UK)

The **ami** consortium comprised both experts in software measurement and users applying quantitative approaches to the management of their projects.

A key contribution to the value of the **ami** method is its validation in practice on a range of projects. The **ami** project included real, full-scale projects which applied the method either to set up new metrics programmes or to develop and refocus existing programmes. Important feedback was provided by these validation projects. There were a total of 19 validation projects covering a wide range of different types and sizes of project and application. The validation was organized by Kevin Pulford (GEC–Marconi), Sheena Bassett (GEC–Marconi), Werner Philip (RWTÜV) and Herbert Schippers (RWTÜV). These projects and their feedback were used extensively to provide practical advice and as a source of illustrations and examples.

The development of the **ami** method and this book has been a complex collaborative exercise. The editorial team, Annie Kuntzmann-Combelles (Objectif Technologie), Kevin Pulford (GEC–Marconi), and Stephen Shirlaw (GEC–Alsthom), who have written and edited the book, wish to thank all those who have contributed. Members of the team who have made major contributions to the book include Peter Comer (O.GROUP), Jacqueline Holdsworth (South Bank University), Norbert Fuchs (ALCATEL), Ulrich Heitkötter (RWTÜV), Ros Herman (South Bank University), Christophe Debou (ALCATEL), Norbert Plan (Objectif Technologie), Alison Rowe (South Bank University) and Robin Whitty (South Bank University).

The **ami** User Group

An **ami** User Group has been set up to exchange experience on the use and application of the **ami** method and to further develop the method. Should you wish to make contact with the **ami** user group or a member of the **ami** consortium the following are the main **ami** contacts.

Lead Partner

GEC–Marconi Software Systems
(UK) [†]
Elstree Way
Borehamwood
Herfordshire WD6 1RX

Contact: Kevin Pulford
Tel: +44 181 732 0705
Fax: +44 181 732 0365

Other Partners

Alcatel Network Systems (Belgium) [†]

Excelsiorlaan 71
B-1930 Zaventem

Contact: Christophe Debou
Tel: +32 2 718 75 11
Fax: +32 2 718 77 98

Bull AG (Germany)

Roger-Bosh-Strasse 52
6070 Langen

Contact: Herr H Mosel
Tel: +49 6103 761374
Fax: +49 6103 761628

[†] National contact points for **ami**.
[‡] International contact point for the **ami** User Group.

GEC–Alsthom Transport SA (France)

Signalling Group
33 Rue des Batieliers
93404 SAINT-OUEN Cedex

Contact: Dr G Guiho
Tel: +33 1 40 10 63 89
Fax: +33 1 40 10 65 06

TECNOS (Grupo SGS CIAT) (Spain) [†]

Piquer 7
28033 Madrid

Contact: Juan Carlos Moreno
Tel: +34 1 766 5333
Fax: +34 1 766 0609

O.Group srl (Italy) [†]

Via Benedetto Croce 19
00142 Roma

Contact: Loredarna Manchini
Tel: +39 65411552
Fax: +39 65415239

Objectif Technologie (France) [†]

31 Avenue du General Leclerc
92340 Bourg-la-Reine

Contact: Annie Kuntzemann-
Combelles
Tel: +33 1 46 64 86 86
Fax: +33 1 46 64 77 39

RWTÜV eV (Germany) [†]

Institute for Information
Technology (IIT)
Im Teelbruch 122
W-4300 Essen 18

Contact: Herbert Schippers
Tel: +49 201 8255120
Fax: +49 201 8255131

South Bank University (UK) [‡]

Centre for Systems and Software
Engineering
School of Computing, Information
Systems and Mathematics
103 Borough Road
London SE1 0AA

Contact: Alison Rowe
Tel: +44 171 815 7504
Fax: +44 171 928 1284

Contents

A Quantitative Approach to Software Management

Chapter 1

Why is measurement so important?

All areas of business and industry use quantitative approaches to management. Measurement is integrated into many performance evaluation, estimation and quality improvement techniques. These techniques are characterized by their emphasis on objectivity and understanding. Problems and results become more apparent to managers, and objectives are clearer to engineers.

The effectiveness of these techniques is well documented. They have given proven benefits to a large number of organizations in the US, in Europe and especially in Japan, where they have been used by software engineers and project managers to produce software of the required quality, on time, within budget and with minimum rework.

The application of quantitative process management and quality improvement techniques to software projects addresses the continuing symptoms of the software crisis: budget and schedule overruns, reliability and quality problems, and the high cost of quality. This cost, the proportion of effort allocated to reviews, corrections, testing and maintenance, is significant and often underestimated. Symptoms of this software crisis are now regularly reported in the press. Some well-known examples are summarized below:

- The director of Ashton Tate pushed for the release of a new version of the company's main database product not realizing that it was full of errors. The product was subsequently recalled. The consequent financial difficulties resulted in the director resigning and the takeover of Ashton Tate by Borland.

- Microsoft had a similar problem with version 4 of its MS-DOS product. So, for version 5, they used 7500 test sites, increasing the cost of quality.

- During the Gulf War, a Scud missile landed on an American army barracks killing several soldiers. A software error in the Patriot missile system had let the Scud pass undetected.

A recent issue of *Business Week* (1991) gives further examples of these sorts of problems.

If you are working in the area of software development you will almost certainly know of other examples. They are not new, and the software crisis was identified over 20 years ago. Although the situation has improved, problems remain, and meanwhile customers are becoming more technology-literate, sophisticated and ready to shop around.

As the above examples show, it is necessary to ensure visibility and to think quantitatively. In other words, everyone must know what is going on in objective terms. How much longer will it take? How many errors are being detected? How much testing has been done? How much did it cost?

Once you know where you are starting from, it is possible to improve estimates and performance. If you are using or choosing methods and tools, investment costs, benefits and problem areas also need to be explicitly stated. Software projects are as much a management and quality management problem as a technical problem.

Examples of the use of metrics

There is growing awareness within the software industry of the benefits of using quantitative goals. Companies such as Hewlett-Packard and Hitachi have been using measurement for some time, and as a result they now produce more reliable software and have become more productive. Large corporations applying measurement do so because they think of software in cost and quality terms. They apply the same quantitative techniques to their software projects as they do to their other business and industrial operations. Figure 1.1 illustrates Hewlett-Packard's success in reducing year-on-year defect rates (Metkit, 1992).

Many companies start measurement by creating a database of project costs and size. The first goal is to improve estimates, but these databases can be used later to evaluate improvements. Some such databases are published and publicly available. An example is the database used for validating the ADA COCOMO cost model (Table 1.1).

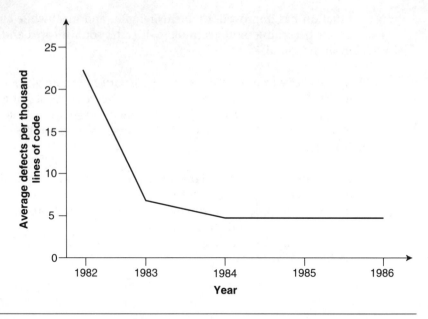

Figure 1.1 An example of quality improvement as a quantitative goal.

Table 1.1 The data used for validating the ADA COCOMO cost model (Boehm, 1989).

Project	Developed size (in non-comment source lines)	Cost (in man-months)	Project duration (in months)	Productivity (in source lines/ man-months)
X	44,000	179	16	245
Y	30,000	107	16	280
A	35,700	119	14	300
B	18,300	78	15	234
C	55,400	337	20	164

Another starting point is the use of measurement in project management. Figure 1.2 illustrates the use of metrics to achieve visibility of project progress during the coding phase. The earned effort (productive effort) is a metric that shows project progress.

At week 20 the project manager realized that the phase was going out of control (effort started to increase more rapidly than progress), and asked for an investigation into the causes. It was found that the software team were not using valid procedures for estimating the required effort remaining. The use of measurement helped in this case to bring the project under control.

The project manager initially saw that there was a problem and then identified the causes. Without the use of metrics the problem would have been detected much later because of the lack of visibility.

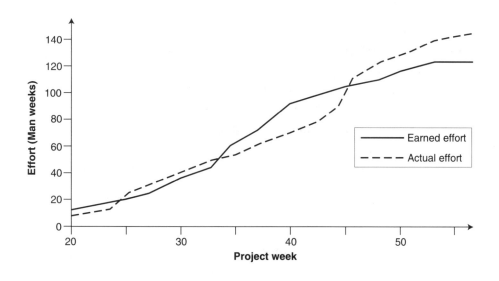

Figure 1.2   The relationship between earned value and costs against time.

Figure 1.3 shows the use of measurement during test phases. The four validation phases are monitored to help decide if the software can be released.

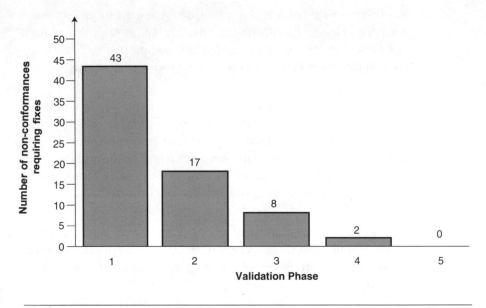

Figure 1.3 The use of measurement during test phases.

Measurement and the **ami** approach

The **ami** approach provides a common-sense framework for quantifying software projects. This framework comprises four activities:

(1) *Assessment* of your environment to link measurement to objectives.

(2) *Analysis* of the assessment conclusions to identify the most suitable metrics.

(3) *Metrication* by implementing a measurement plan.

(4) *Improvement* as you exploit the measurement data and implement actions.

The main benefit of the **ami** approach is that it is a tried and tested method which couples the use of metrics to the achievement and improvement of organizational objectives. It allows you to identify the goals of the decision makers so that measurement will be productively exploited. It is also iterative. You will currently have a certain level of understanding and mastery of your software process. As you start to make use of measurement, your understanding will increase and your goals will become more focused.

The business perspective

Many companies are now enjoying the benefits of having defined business goals and mission statements. By making these goals and objectives public, managers have engaged the synergy of their people, and are obtaining active participation in business improvement programmes. Staff have a clearer picture of what the enterprise is setting out to achieve, and how they are able to contribute. They no longer feel their best efforts are being squandered.

Already, within the organization, quantitative approaches are commonplace for communicating management goals and obtaining early warning of problems. The most important instance is the budgeting process which is one of the major events in the business cycle. Goals for profit, period costs, staffing and salaries are used to direct activity across the organization. Tracking of progress against financial targets is one example of how measurement at the process level is aggregated and summarized to provide decision makers with a clear picture of variations, opportunities and risks.

Project and process measurement which is relevant and significant to the organization complements the information portfolio of the decision makers. It is likely that much of the measurement data you need already exists on shelves and in filing cabinets. Project members routinely fill in time sheets, change control and problem reports. A quick audit will uncover just how much of this information exists. Why not put it to good use? After all, you are already paying for it.

How can I justify the cost?

One of the many questions asked about quantifying software production is 'How can I justify the cost?' While you think about this question, perhaps you can supply the following information:

(1) How much does your current budgeting process cost?

(2) How much value does it add? To you? Your customers? Your staff?

(3) What would be the cost of not having a budget?

(4) Which three activities contribute most to budgeting costs?

(5)   Have you applied process improvement to your budgeting process?

(6)   How could you improve the efficiency of your budgeting process by 10%?

(7)   What savings would you obtain?

(8)   Do you really want to know where the money is going in your software production department?

(9)   Do you really want satisfied customers?

(10) How much are these last two worth to you?

If you answered 'yes' to questions 8 and 9, read on.

The benefits of measurement

Measurement that is used for both the control and improvement of software projects gives the following benefits:

- *Planning, managing and monitoring projects*: Measurement enables increased visibility of the quality and progress of a project. Use of data improves predictions and evaluations. Goal orientation improves project coordination.

- *Matching the software development process to business objectives*: Better matching of the software development process to business objectives can lead to improved confidence between you and your customer, between business managers and project managers and between the Software Development Department and the rest of the organization.

- *Implementing of quality and productivity improvement programmes*: The problem of managing investment in software engineering activities is becoming increasingly important. Such investment may be in 'preventive' activities such as use of methods, quality assurance, increased training and more testing, or in 'productive' activities enabled by CASE tools and new technologies. Measurement helps you to justify, manage and evaluate such improvement programmes. It also helps you to have an improved understanding of problems so you can reach your targets. The **ami** approach (Assess, Analyse, Metricate, Improve) is an adaptation of Deming's widely used

Plan–Do–Check–Act cycle (Deming, 1982) for improvement using software measurement.

- *Aiding communication*: Measurement goals are as much about communication as they are about evaluations and targets. For example, the Software Development Department might rely on a Systems Department for running and maintaining the host development computers. Measuring resource use or the cost of inefficient practices can help the dialogue between the two departments, because measurement gives an objective framework for this communication.

To achieve full benefits, measurement must first be applied systematically. The iterative **ami** approach is based on common sense and standard management techniques. As you read this book you will find the method for applying this approach to software projects presented in a readily usable format.

This book will also act as a focal point to help you and your organization to use software measurement effectively. Measurement involves many people. For instance, managers will give goals, team leaders will interpret the measurement data, an engineer will write the measurement plan and other engineers will collect the data. The **ami** approach will help to structure activities and roles.

The approach has been tested with good results on software projects at sites throughout Europe. Most importantly, it reflects both standard techniques used in many areas of business and industry as well as best practice in software development. You will find that leading companies are giving examples of the uses of measurement on software projects and are also claiming important benefits (see Moeuller (1992), Chapter 7). They all advise that a systematic approach is used.

Do not wait to get started until everybody reports (and already profits from) the benefits. We recommend that you try out this approach simply because it reflects good practice and has been shown to work by the results of documented tests on a wide variety of software projects throughout Europe.

Applying the **ami** Approach

During software development all the participants, whether designers, testers or management, make decisions. Decision making implies goals. The objective of measurement is to make data available to decision makers in order to support the achievement of these goals.

The activity of software development (such as maintenance, installation, etc.) is a process. Within the process we can identify tasks, identify the resources used and the output produced. But development is made up both of formalized procedures and of mental activities such as decision making, creative design, management and the application of technology. There is a link from goals and decision making to the measurable entities (resources, processes, products) of your project.

The link is the participants, because the primary goals for measurement can be traced to the participants involved in the process. This link takes the form of a tree of sub-goals, so it is possible to trace the metrics that are used to characterize the project back to primary goals.

This approach is called ***goal-oriented measurement***.

Summary of the **ami** method

The application of goal-oriented measurement in an organization requires a structured method. Each organization, because it is different from all other organizations, must construct its own measurement framework. Which organization, after all, would borrow the mission statement of another?

Without a method, it is not possible to build a coherent framework and the result does not reflect real needs. The organization wastes a lot of time discovering and trying out more or less successful methods but, out of frustration, measurement is often abandoned before a method is allowed to take root.

The **ami** method implements four distinct activities – Assess, Analyse, Metricate, Improve:

(1) *Assess* your project environment (with its objectives and problems) to define primary goals for measurement. Managers who initiate measurement must be involved in this activity.

(2) *Analyse* the primary goals to derive sub-goals and the relevant metrics. This analysis is formalized as a goal tree with a corresponding set of questions to which these metrics are linked. The participants affected by the metrication goals (metrics promoter, project managers, quality engineers, etc.) will generally carry out this activity.

(3) *Metricate* by implementing a measurement plan and then process the collected primitive data into measurement data. The metrics promoter will write the measurement plan and coordinate its implementation.

(4) *Improve*, as the participants affected by the goals start to use the measurement data and implement actions. Comparison of the measurement data with the goals and questions in the measurement plan will guide you towards achievement of your immediate project goals. When your measurements show that you have achieved a goal, you have improved enough to reassess your primary goals.

The relationship between the four activities is shown in Figure 2.1. The method is a 12-step sequence with a series of support tools (guidelines, templates and examples) to make it easy to use. How these steps implement the four activities is illustrated in Figure 2.2.

Getting started

There are five important prerequisites for successful use of the method.

(1) Managers must be involved. Control and improvement (and goal-oriented measurement) cannot be brought in as if it were simply a tool. Management must take the lead in initiating measurement, defining goals and asking for the feedback information.

(2) Measurement tasks must be clearly allocated and budgeted so that all those concerned will be able to put in the required effort.

(3) There must be a metrics promoter to write and implement the measurement plan and to organize the presentation and distribution of the information. His or her main role is to keep everyone involved in the metrication process. The analysis of

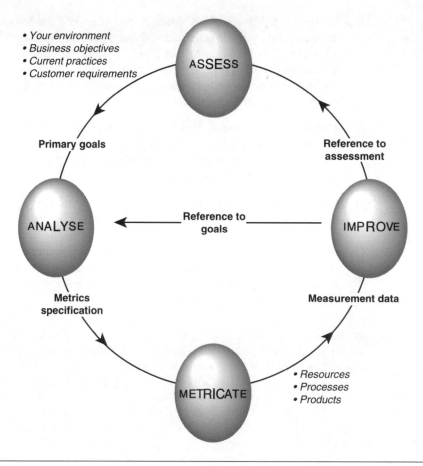

- Your environment
- Business objectives
- Current practices
- Customer requirements

ASSESS

Primary goals

Reference to assessment

ANALYSE

Reference to goals

IMPROVE

Metrics specification

Measurement data

METRICATE

- Resources
- Processes
- Products

Figure 2.1 The relationship between the four **ami** activities.

measurement data should relate to the needs of participants affected by the goals (project managers, designers, etc.).

(4)   There must be a work environment in which goal-oriented measurement is feasible. The essential criterion is not project size or maturity level but continuity of management strategy. There is little point in investing in an improvement programme if there is no element of continuity between projects.

(5)   Don't forget training. Measurement in the workplace is an emotive issue for all members of staff. Typically the initial reaction is, 'You can't measure software production'. Another common reaction is fear – fear of having your customary working practices subjected to scrutiny and laid bare to criticism.

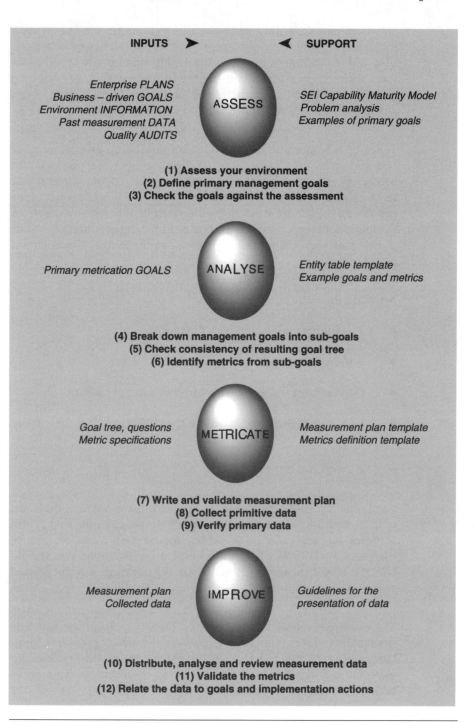

INPUTS ➤   ◄ SUPPORT

Enterprise PLANS
Business – driven GOALS
Environment INFORMATION
Past measurement DATA
Quality AUDITS

ASSESS

SEI Capability Maturity Model
Problem analysis
Examples of primary goals

(1) Assess your environment
(2) Define primary management goals
(3) Check the goals against the assessment

Primary metrication GOALS

ANALYSE

Entity table template
Example goals and metrics

(4) Break down management goals into sub-goals
(5) Check consistency of resulting goal tree
(6) Identify metrics from sub-goals

Goal tree, questions
Metric specifications

METRICATE

Measurement plan template
Metrics definition template

(7) Write and validate measurement plan
(8) Collect primitive data
(9) Verify primary data

Measurement plan
Collected data

IMPROVE

Guidelines for the
presentation of data

(10) Distribute, analyse and review measurement data
(11) Validate the metrics
(12) Relate the data to goals and implementation actions

Figure 2.2 The 12 steps of the **ami** method.

However sound, well-thought-out and well-intentioned your plans for implementing measurement, they stand or fall by the collaboration and commitment of your staff. Unless you openly involve and train your staff at all stages during the implementation of your own programme, your investment and best efforts are wasted. Even worse, staff morale and staff's trust in you is damaged.

Training is important to get your programme up and running as fast and effectively as possible. The **ami** project has produced an integrated set of educational modules that enable professional teachers and trainers to build courses of varying lengths concentrating on different aspects of software engineering measurement for students, software engineers and managers. (Of particular relevance is the **ami** training module 'How to implement a measurement programme'.)

Now, ask these questions:

● Do you have managers' involvement?

● Is there a budget?

● Do you have someone who can be a metrics champion?

● Is there sufficient consensus on the strategy that it will remain unchanged for long enough?

● Is there commitment to training?

Goal-oriented measurement is an iterative cycle but this does not help in deciding where to get started. A simple example that is also a useful starting point is presented in the Fast Track sections of Chapters 3 to 6. Once you have studied the example, you should select the best means by which your organization can get started with the **ami** method.

The example is taken from goals and metrics in common use. The main sources for this are the members of the **ami** consortium. Similar examples can be found from the experience of Hewlett-Packard as recounted by Grady and Caswell (1987) or from the experiences of Siemens and Data Logic as presented in Moeuller (1992).

Setting up the metrics team

All organizations are different and the particular approach and methodology adopted for the measurement initiative will be peculiar to the organization. Here is a simple model that we found useful on the **ami** project. It should be possible to adapt this model to your own situation and it should give you an idea of what is needed in terms of setting up a team to support the initiative.

The main player in the initiative is what we call the metrics initiator and is likely to be a senior manager with sufficient financial responsibility to allocate a budget for use on a measurement programme. He or she will typically have several projects under his or her control and will be responsible for the organization of the measurement programme although not necessarily the person who does most of the actual work. The metrics initiator is likely to be the person who will justify the programme in business terms.

The metrics promoter reports to the metrics initiator and is responsible for the coordination and organization of the measurement initiative on a day-to-day basis. He or she is the person responsible for coordinating execution of the steps, writing the measurement plan, implementing and supervising data collection, and writing analysis reports. To do this he or she will require input from the projects to help in putting together the goals and measurement plan for the initiative. The metrics promoter should have some experience of the use and application of metrics, and be familiar with the problems of interpreting the results of metrics collection.

The other participants in the initiative will be drawn from the projects and will include project managers, team leaders and project quality engineers. They will be involved in the definition of goals and in the interpretation of data. All participants, including engineers, will be involved in data collection.

Costs and benefits

It is important to look at metrication costs so that measurement can be correctly planned and evaluated. Costs are much the same as equivalent management and quality procedures that generate and report data, and can be estimated by looking at the various measurement tasks and the resources involved.

The following will give you some idea of what is involved in the main tasks in a goal-oriented approach to help you estimate the level of costs that might be incurred in your measurement programme:

- *Assessment of the project's environment.* A small assessment team will be set up. The size of this team will depend on the size of the organization being assessed. The team will need to talk to the project managers and quality engineers. A report summarizing their findings will be produced by the metrics promoter.

- *Definition of primary goals.* The metrics promoter will discuss the results of the environment assessment and the setting of goals with the metrics initiator. There may need to be several meetings to achieve a consensus on the goals to be adopted for the measurement programme.

- *Derivation of sub-goals and metrics.* A number of meetings will be needed with the project management and team leaders to identify the appropriate sub-goals and questions, and then to identify the metrics to support these.

- *Writing the measurement plan and designing collection forms.* The metrics promoter will be responsible for the compilation of the plan. The amount of work involved is related to the number of metrics that will be collected and the degree of detail in the plan.

- *Data collection.* Data will normally be collected by the engineers working on the project and be collated either at project level or centrally by the metrics promoter. The level of effort is related to the amount of data to be collected and the ease with which it is available.

- *Data analysis.* The metrics promoter will prepare the presentation of the results. The level of effort will depend on the frequency at which reports are produced and the number of managers they need to be discussed with.

- *Goals and assessment review.* The metrics promoter will produce a report for consideration by the metrics initiator and the participants, which will be discussed with the relevant managers to assess the significance of the results. This might be done on a one-to-one basis between the metrics promoter and individual managers or in a meeting of all managers. The level of effort will depend on the way these meetings are organized and their frequency. The result of these meetings should be an action plan that will lead to another loop of the **ami** method.

Six factors can cause variations in these costs:

(1) *The level of data collection already present*: before embarking on a metrication programme, it is worth looking at existing data collection costs. Most companies collect some data. One example is project management data such as effort spent on different project modules and effort spent correcting and maintaining software. Another source is quality control data relating to the number of modifications requested or to the quality level achieved.

(2) *Organizations with visible and controlled development processes have reduced costs*: if they are certified for ISO 9001 or have a well-defined process, organizations will normally have procedures in place that can be used in measurement data analysis. Examples include project reviews, change control procedures and quality control activities.

(3) *The more metrics for which data is collected, the greater the cost*: the more metrics are used, the more issues are covered, with a corresponding increase in implementation and analysis costs. However, it is possible to build up over time a useful set of metrics without excessively increasing costs. This is achieved by automating key data collection and analysis activities. Goal-oriented measurement is used to target key metrics and avoid excessive data collection.

(4) *There is a 'trial and error' learning curve to introducing a measurement strategy into the software development process*: these 'trial and error' costs can be minimized by using this book. It is described in a structured sequence that has been designed and thoroughly proven to contain the essential but necessary actions required for a successful measurement programme.

(5) *Monitoring the initiative itself helps control the costs associated with it and leads to the programme becoming more cost effective*: the objectives, results and costs of measurement should be monitored. The **ami** method has to prove its effectiveness throughout the measurement initiative. This can be measured through a self-assessment approach based, for example, on participant satisfaction, initiator satisfaction, comparison between cost of measurement and cost of project management, number and importance of the decisions made. When starting the initiative, quantitative indicators should

be defined which will demonstrate the effectiveness of the **ami** approach. These can be used to show the degree of acceptance of the approach in the company and the economic benefits of the metrics process.

(6) *Suitability of goals and metrics*: this is the most important influencing factor on your costs. If you select over-ambitious goals and metrics, not suited to your needs and process maturity level, the metrication costs may increase rapidly. Using **ami** helps you to find appropriate goals and an acceptable cost level.

Although there is a clear investment in quantifying software projects, two points should be noted. Use of goal-oriented measurement leads to predictable and controlled metrication costs. This cost is likely not to be as great as it first might appear since collecting metrics data is only an extension of your existing data collection activities.

Costs are kept to a minimum. With the **ami** method, the number of metrics that need to be collected is focused on those that correspond to the more important goals. Thus data collection and analysis costs can be limited to the metrics which give the best return. Moreover, since the goal is identified and the metrics are derived from the goal, there is a certain latitude to choose metrics that are easier and less expensive to collect. Finally, entry costs do not have to be high. When you are starting to use the method, it is best to restrict the number of goals to about two or three.

The emphasis on goals and business objectives establishes a clear link to strategic business decisions. There is a reduced risk of unprofitable measurement and of excessive data overloads hampering the decision-making process. The clear definition of goals helps in the acceptance of measurement by team leaders and engineers. They can be naturally suspicious of measurement that is collected for unspecified reasons and can be demotivated by measurement that is not clearly put to good use.

Specific cost and benefits figures

Although there are various factors affecting metrication costs, here are some statistics from the **ami** validation projects that give an idea of the costs and the benefits. These validation projects were real, industrial projects which applied the **ami** method.

The average cost for the metrication of a project using the **ami** approach was found to be 2–5% of the total cost for the software development. This is the initial cost for the first **ami** loop. If you apply a similar plan for further projects, the cost will decrease to 1–3%. The following example comes from an **ami** validation project.

The company used **ami** and defined long-term goals related to the control and improvement of productivity and cost estimations. These projects involved a series of upgrades of clerical applications which consisted of about 2500 modules. The cost of the measurement initiative for the first upgrade project was 6.5% of the cost of the upgrade. When applied to the fourth upgrade the cost decreased to 1%. Table 2.1 gives the main figures for the project.

Table 2.1 Decreasing cost of applying the **ami** method.

Upgrade	Metrication cost (as % of total)	No. of primitive data items collected	Cost of planning steps to collection and analysis steps
First	6.5	61	40/60
Second	5.5	61	15/85
Third	2.0	61	5/95
Fourth	1.0	61	3/97

In general all the benefits cannot be measured in terms of cost. Some benefits are indirect such as greater customer satisfaction from improved product quality. Benefits reported by the **ami** validation projects include:

- measuring the effectiveness of a new testing tool demonstrated that it did not provide the advantages looked for;

- better project control through improved process visibility;

- understanding of the impact of OOA/OOD (Object-Oriented Analysis/Object-Oriented Design) methodologies on the software life cycle;

- identification of critical parts of the development process upon which to concentrate quality assessment (QA) activities;

- improvement of cost prediction by a better understanding of the cost influence factors;

- improvement of productivity through determination and control of important process and product characteristics;

- better knowledge of the maintenance process.

Use of this book

This book presents the method in an easy-to-use format. Chapters 3 to 6 give a complete 'how to do it' presentation of the **ami** method. Each of these chapters starts with 'fast-track pages' which give a simplified summary of the material in the chapter. These pages are targeted at those who have little experience of metrication or insufficient time to read the whole book. A simple example is included that will help you see how the method is applied. If you have enough time, read the whole chapter so as to understand each activity and to define your own goals and metrics.

Within Chapters 3 to 6 the detailed step-by-step descriptions enable you to apply the method for yourself. These detailed descriptions include examples from the practical experience of the **ami** consortium on its software validation projects. The chapters are organized around the major activities of the **ami** method.

Chapter 3, 'Defining the Primary Goals', discusses issues in the assessment of the development environment so as to define primary goals for metrication. This chapter is especially useful to managers who are responsible for defining the software development strategy of an organization. A particular assessment procedure is discussed in detail in Appendix 1, the SEI assessment.

Chapter 4, 'Deriving Metrics', shows how to analyse the primary goals to derive the metrics. This activity will normally be performed by a small group, one of whom will then write the measurement plan. A basic set of metrics is available in Appendix 3.

Chapter 5, 'Implementing a Measurement Plan', presents a template for writing the plan and gives advice on implementation and data collection. It is aimed at the metrics promoter who has the task of developing and implementing the measurement plan. Users of the metrics plan, such as managers and data collectors, will also find this chapter useful.

Chapter 6, 'Exploiting Your Measures', discusses ways in which the measurement effort can be effectively exploited and is of general interest, and Chapter 7 gives a list of sources and suggested further reading. Measurement cannot be conducted independently of other activities, so it is useful to understand the links.

Appendix 1 describes the SEI process assessment; Appendix 2 gives some example of goals and metrics; Appendix 3 gives a list of some common metrics; and Appendix 4 gives further case studies of the application of the **ami** method.

A glossary of the main terms used in this book will be found at the end of the book.

A running example

We will be using a simple example to illustrate how to apply the **ami** method. It is loosely based on one of the **ami** validation projects but has been slightly changed to allow us to bring out features of the method that would not have been brought out otherwise. For convenience we have called this the Guinea Pig Project.

The Guinea Pig Project was in its maintenance phase. It had implementations on two platforms; this is reflected in the project structure which has two separate teams looking after the software for each platform. The project structure is shown in Figure 2.3. You will see that this is a small project in terms of the number of engineers involved.

The updates to the software are designed, coded and unit tested by the appropriate development team. It is then handed over to the Integration team to perform the integration testing and acceptance tests.

The motivation behind the implementation of a measurement programme in the Guinea Pig Project was as follows. The Divisional Manager and the Guinea Pig Project Manager were getting increasingly uneasy about the level of quality of the delivered software. They were getting a large number of errors reported after delivery to the customer. This was also causing a lot of effort to be spent on reworking the software to fix the problems. The management were looking to a measurement programme to help them control the level of quality of the delivered software.

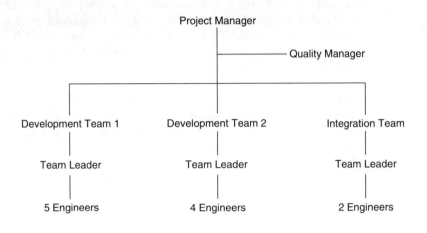

Figure 2.3 Guinea Pig Project structure.

Having decided to use the **ami** method to put their measurement programme into place, the management's next decision was to appoint a Metrics Promoter. They could get in a consultant or appoint someone from within the company or the project. They elected to appoint someone from within the company but not from the project so that they could devote sufficient time to the measurement programme. The Metrics Promoter was a senior engineer familiar with the organization of the company and an understanding of how projects are run.

The Metrics Promoter's first action was to get up to speed by going on an **ami** training course and reading the handbook. Having become familiar with the **ami** method and the concerns of the management in relation to the Guinea Pig Project, the Metrics Promoter then planned how he would tackle the implementation of the **ami** method. What they ended up doing is the subject of the example sections in subsequent chapters.

Recommendations

Here are a few general recommendations, most of them from the **ami** validation projects, that will help you to set up a successful measurement programme.

- *Get support and commitment.* Don't start an extensive metrication programme if you don't have the commitment and support of your managers.

- *Don't try to progress too quickly.* Start with a simple programme and build up.

- *Take care of psychological aspects.*
  - Ensure that all the people involved in metrication and are properly motivated and trained.
  - Never promote 'metrics use'; promote a solution to a need.

- *Estimate planning and budget.*

  - Include measurement as part of the planning of your project.
  - Set up specific project procedures for metrics activities and ensure they are used.
  - Allow enough resources; doing the job on the cheap will not work.

Defining the Primary Goals

In this chapter we see how to assess the project environment in order to define and evaluate primary goals for subsequent metrication. These primary goals may be business-driven or may evolve more directly from the project environment.

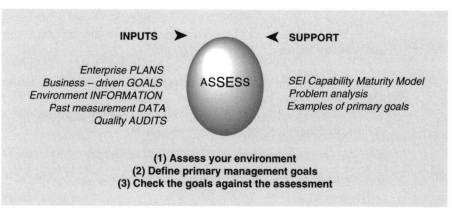

INPUTS ➤   ◄ SUPPORT

Enterprise PLANS
Business – driven GOALS   ASSESS   SEI Capability Maturity Model
Environment INFORMATION   Problem analysis
Past measurement DATA   Examples of primary goals
Quality AUDITS

(1) Assess your environment
(2) Define primary management goals
(3) Check the goals against the assessment

ami steps 1–3

Chapter 3

Fast track

Plan of action

It is vital that the strategic decision to develop and implement a software measurement plan is taken by management. Managers must also be fully involved in the examination of assessment data and in the definition of primary goals for metrication.

Areas of concern and problems in the way in which your organization currently responds to business and customer needs must first be identified.

A procedure and model, such as the SEI Capability Maturity Model from the Software Engineering Institute of Carnegie Mellon University, is helpful in the assessment process. (This is described in detail in Appendix 1.) The capability maturity level can be used to guide the choice of primary goals. You measure to increase your understanding. You always link metrication goals to your present level of understanding.

Alternatively, a localized procedure for problem identification and analysis can be used.

Either of these methods enables you to produce a list of issues. These are then assessed to identify the key items to be tackled first, which in turn leads to the definition of the primary goals for metrication. In other words it is essential to know:

- Where are you starting from? (your current position)
- Where do you want to go? (your target position)

The first activity of the **ami** approach helps you answer the above two questions. It is important to define primary goals, otherwise time and effort are wasted. Studies have shown that many attempts at implementing measurement plans have failed through lack of either clear or valid goals. The above two questions are dependent on each other. When assessing a situation, you may discover difficulties, and after analysis, you will be able to define a goal to either control the situation in the short term or improve it in the medium term.

Your primary goals should always be checked against your assessment conclusions to confirm the link between the two questions.

Making it easy: one step at a time

As an example we can look at primary goals definition using the SEI Capability Maturity Model. The model suggests the following approach:

(1)   Start with the measurement of the progress and results of projects, in terms of a few simple metrics.

(2)   Measure product characteristics and all problem areas to help define a suitable development process.

(3)   Measure the characteristics of the process you have defined.

(4)   Automate the measurement environment to achieve in-depth continuous control of the process.

Using this procedure, the Software Engineering Institute (SEI) has already assessed hundreds of sites and projects against the model. Over 85% of these projects needed to improve initial key software engineering practices, including the area of software measurement. A common assessment conclusion is that there is very little quantification of projects.

So, begin with the measurement of progress and project results in terms of a few simple metrics; then, define the primary goals to match the assessment conclusion (Figure 3.1). Examples of matching primary goals are:

●   monitoring project productivity

●   improving estimates

●   improving product reliability

●   assessing visibility of project quality

●   supporting project management with data from past projects

These goals are often a good starting point for a first measurement plan, and we shall be tracking these examples for you throughout the fast-track pages of this book. You can simply take these examples and begin working with them straight away. However, the SEI model looks essentially at engineering and software management procedures, and there are other important viewpoints on your process and its inputs and outputs that you should consider. The following sections discuss in more detail how to do your own assessment and how to define your own primary goals.

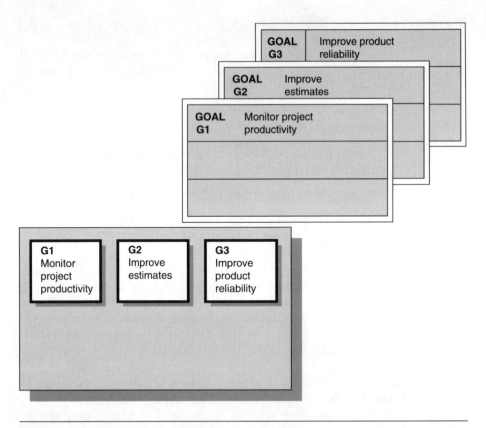

Figure 3.1 Definition of primary goals.

Step 1: Assessing your environment

Assessment is the first step of the **ami** method. It is evident from experience that there is more than one procedure for assessing the environment of a company or a team. Assessment is a general activity of collecting, examining and sorting information to arrive at a judgement. Typically judgements will be made of such things as areas of risk and maturity of software management practice. The conclusions of this assessment are used in the second step of the **ami** method as an aid to the definition of primary goals.

Assessment can utilize a variety of sources of information such as enterprise plans, past measurement data or other information on your company's commercial activities and quality management processes. These can be supplemented by audits, problem analysis, reviews of existing documentation and SEI capability maturity assessment. In-house guidelines for audits, assessments, project reviews, and measurement programmes should all be used as a support for Step 1.

The assessment procedure involves an examination of the environment from one or more viewpoints:

- *Process viewpoint*: this consists of elementary activities such as scheduling, roles and responsibilities. This is the viewpoint used in the SEI procedure that is developed in the next section.

- *Product viewpoint*: an analysis of the product characteristics against quality criteria. This type of viewpoint is generally customer-oriented.

- *Communications viewpoint*: this is the network of information exchanged between team members.

Each of these viewpoints is important enough to be worth consideration. There are several possible approaches to using any of these viewpoints and you can even consider several viewpoints together. The viewpoints selected for assessment will depend on the decision-making responsibility of the initiator.

The **ami** approach recommends a process viewpoint to assess the environment for two reasons. Firstly, the **ami** validation projects proved the usefulness of this type of assessment procedure and secondly, the development process gives meaningful measures and determines the quality of the product.

Below we give two approaches to assessment, namely, the SEI Capability Maturity Model and problem analysis. The SEI Capability Maturity Model is the one recommended in the **ami** approach. It is one of the most widely used procedures for the evaluation of development process and organization for software production. However, problem analysis and the SEI Capability Maturity Model can be used together and will yield complementary and supportive information.

SEI assessment

The aim of SEI assessment is to assess the software development maturity of companies. The assessment is part of a procedure for the

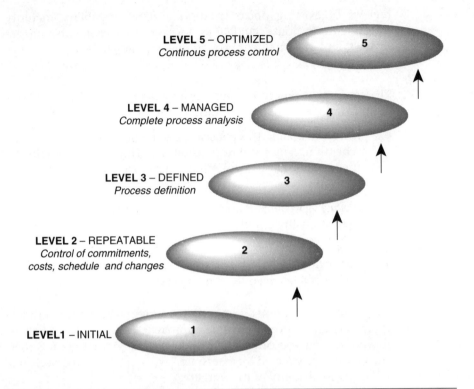

LEVEL 5 – OPTIMIZED
Continous process control

LEVEL 4 – MANAGED
Complete process analysis

LEVEL 3 – DEFINED
Process definition

LEVEL 2 – REPEATABLE
*Control of commitments,
costs, schedule and changes*

LEVEL1 – INITIAL

Figure 3.2   The five levels of software maturity.

Software Capability Evaluation (SCE) of contractors working for the US Department of Defense. It has consequently been widely disseminated and practised. The assessment procedure developed by the Software Engineering Institute (SEI) of Carnegie Mellon University is described in detail in Appendix 1.

SEI assessment is based on a five-level model (see Figure 3.2) of the process of software development. The results of the SEI assessment can be complemented by product and communications analysis to get a full picture of the software production within a group. The usefulness of the additional information depends on the management strategy for measurement. Most organizations are at level 1. Very few have reached level 5, and the remainder are mainly spread between levels 2 and 3.

●   *Level 1 – Initial*: the process is unstable and disorganized. No orderly progress in improving the process is possible until the process is under a repeatable level of control.

- *Level 2 – Repeatable*: the organization has a process with a repeatable level of regular control by instigating rigorous project management of commitments, costs, schedules and changes.

- *Level 3 – Defined*: the organization has defined its process firstly to ensure consistent implementation, and secondly to provide a model on which to build a better understanding. At this point new process technology can be introduced in a controlled way.

- *Level 4 – Managed*: the organization has initiated comprehensive and detailed process measurements. The process is reasonably well controlled. Regular analysis of all the collected data is carried out and the results fed into the decision-making system.

- *Level 5 – Optimized*: data collection and analysis is an integral part of the process. Management routinely evaluates the performance of the projects, and the effect of changes in the process introduced to improve the performance.

The assessment procedure comprises a set of questions, each corresponding to the various main areas of software engineering practice. A 'yes' answer to a question is related to one of four maturity levels 2 to 5. A 'no' answer is rated at the initial level 1. This questionnaire makes it easy for you to assess the maturity of your software development process. You will then be able to identify the steps needed to control and improve the software process.

Problem analysis

By identifying problems on past projects you will be able to identify areas of your development process that need attention and improvement. The objective of problem analysis is to identify the problems and their background to serve as a basis for setting the goals.

At any level, whatever project, department or company, various types of problems may be apparent. As has been pointed out above, problem analysis can be an alternative or a complement to the SEI capability assessment. Problem identification is a natural complement to the assessment of engineering practice. Typical problems that will be encountered are budget overruns, schedule slippage, excessive number of fault reports and high level of change requests from the customer. To support your problem analysis you can produce a questionnaire to help focus on various key items. The questionnaire is followed up using interviews and other data to determine the state of the company.

These observations might be usefully complemented by analysing communication charts related to the people concerned. Such charts identify communication between people and the type and frequency of the information exchanged, and they may show either a lack of information or the flow of useless information.

We have assumed that the actual reporting mechanism in your organization is sufficient to identify existing problems. In some cases, an audit can be carried out to identify major causes of problems. The **ami** method does not include an auditing procedure, but the conclusions of an audit could be a good starting point for the definition of primary goals for measurement. Through interviews, document reviews and process analysis, an audit will draw a realistic picture of the actual status of your software development practices.

Example: Step 1 for the Guinea Pig Project

We should now be in a position to see how we can apply this step to the Guinea Pig Project and then examine the sorts of decisions that the Metrics Promoter and the management team made. The Guinea Pig Project Manager took on the role of Initiator.

The Metrics Promoter's first decision was how to assess the project's development environment. He elected to use the SEI procedure given in the **ami** handbook since this would give him a good overall view of the project without any prejudice from earlier preconceptions.

The Metrics Promoter knew that the focus of management attention was on the quality of the product and so the assessment would need to take the product viewpoint into account. The management wanted to get the quality of the product up as soon as possible. The Metrics Promoter would have to determine if this was possible and what was the most likely time-scale.

The next question the Metrics Promoter needed to address was how to carry out the assessment. They could do it team-by-team or take the project as a whole. In this case the project was small enough to consider as a whole. The Metrics Promoter conducted the assessment

Table 3.1 Extract from report on the assessment of the Guinea Pig Project.

Question	Answer	Justification
1.1.1	Yes	The project procedures manual includes organization charts that show this.
1.1.2	No	The project is a sub-contract. The overall project manager is within the prime contractor's organization.
1.1.3	No	The project quality engineer reports directly to the project manager.
1.1.6	Yes	The project uses configuration management tools.

The question numbers refer to the question numbers of the SEI questionnaire given in Appendix 1.

by convening a meeting with the Project Manager and the project Quality Manager. The Metrics Promoter read out the questions and noted the answers on the questionnaire. The Project Manager answered from his knowledge of the project and the Quality Manager assessed whether the answer was adequate in the context and against his knowledge of the project's procedures. A certain amount of discussion was necessary on some questions to decide whether the response was a reasonable answer to the spirit of the question.

The result of the assessment was that the project was at level 1. From this the Metrics Promoter knew that the improvement goal would not be appropriate for the Guinea Pig Project and that knowledge goals would be the order of the day.

The results of the assessment were incorporated into a report which included the justification of the replies that were given. An example of part of the report is given in Table 3.1 to give you an idea of its layout and content. The project can use the report when a reassessment is carried out following process improvement

Making it easy: the assessment

Before you start your assessment and select your assessment method it is useful to consider the following which will help to define the scope of your assessment.

- the responsibilities and position of the initiator of the measurement initiative and of the assessment

- the budget allocated for the measurement plan

- the viewpoint of the assessment

- the issues to be addressed

- the problems to be solved

- the milestones and time-scales for problem solving

- the priorities

Once you know where you are, you will be able to think about where you want to go, and you can go on to define primary goals.

Recommendations

- Remember that you are using the SEI questionnaire to help you to understand your development process and identify your problem areas. You must be realistic.

- Do not be tempted into giving over-optimistic scores. You are only misleading yourself.

- Make sure all the participants see the results of your assessment and have the opportunity to comment on them.

- Do not become fixated on the maturity level score – it is only a guide.

Step 2 : Defining primary management goals

Once the reference situation is known, either from an assessment procedure or from an intuitive understanding and investigation of your projects, it is time to define primary goals for metrication. Generally speaking, two classes of goals exist:

(1) *Knowledge goals:* these are expressed by the use of such verbs as evaluate, predict or monitor. The adoption of knowledge goals for metrication means that you want to get a better understanding of your development process and environment and to monitor the effect of changes. For example you may want to assess product quality, obtain data to predict testing

effort, monitor test coverage or monitor requirements changes. Achieving knowledge goals is the necessary primary step before taking decisions to modify your development process.

(2)   *Change or achievement goals:* these are expressed by the use of such verbs as increase, reduce, improve or achieve. The adoption of change goals means that you are aware of shortcomings in your development processes and in your environment and want to improve them.

In implementing a measurement programme there is a natural progression that needs to be followed to achieve success. A measurement programme is likely to be started from strategic company goals such as: improvement of customers' satisfaction, or competitiveness. These need to be converted to goals related to the software development process. Before you can start improving the development process, you need to measure your present performance so that you will have something against which to measure the improvement. Once you have established your baselines, you can consider changing your development process and measure the improvement.

Remember that objectives or goals are statements of the required outcome. They do not describe what you will be measuring.

General goals are translated into action goals. These goals identify the actions the participants (managers, developers, engineers) need to take to achieve the goal. A key step after identifying goals is to translate them into benefits for the participants. A successful measurement plan takes into account the needs of the people involved in measurement. The analysis and knowledge of the participants is consequentially as important as the definition of the goals:

● Who are they?

● What are their expectations?

● Who makes the decisions?

● What do they want to know?

● Are there different levels of participants?

● Are they interested in the results?
– in the process?

● What do they know?
– about measurement?

  – about the software ?
  – about the software process?
  – about how decisions are made?

- Do they want detailed information?

- Do they have constraints of any kind?

Participants will have different viewpoints, responsibilities, senior-ity and background. Consequently, their expectations as to the relevance and urgency of the information collected will also be dif-ferent. The types of participant that are likely to be involved with the measurement programme are:

- *Senior executives*, who are often very short of time. They look at the broadest level of impact and need to make sure that the decisions are in line with corporate directives and make financial sense.

- *Middle-level managers* (that is, project managers and above) are concerned with how the measurement programme will affect their own projects. They are likely to be more interested in assessing particular processes of their development process.

- *Engineers* will need the most detailed information because they will need it to guide their work.

- *Customers* are primarily concerned that the system that is delivered does the job they have specified. They will want to see evidence that their requirements and constraints have been implemented.

Another important factor that will affect the selection of goals is the budget that you allocate to the measurement programme. A limited budget will mean that you cannot afford to have too many goals since this will mean that you would have to use a large amount of effort to collect the large number of metrics required to support the goals.

If you are just starting measurement it will make sense to select only two or three primary goals until you have gained some experi-ence in collecting metrics. This will give you time to learn how to make your measurement programme efficient and have ironed out all the teething problems.

The validation projects experience reported that 'knowledge' goals were most often selected and that the software process maturity rating attained confirmed that 'information seeking' goals would be best in the circumstances. Many projects found it necessary to reduce the number of main goals from an ambitious eight to ten down to two or three to keep to a reasonable level of effort.

Examples of goals

Primary goals are either defined by reference to the situation highlighted by the assessment, or simply recognized intuitively. In all cases, we recommend that the goals are precise, quantitative and formulated in simple and understandable words. Each definition should be one or at most two sentences.

Examples of primary goals related to the SEI capability maturity model are:

● to support project management with process data (to move from level 1)

● to gain a better understanding of project costings (level 1)

● to gain a better understanding of project software quality (level 1)

● to attain an error rate of x errors per 1000 lines of code (level 3)

● to reduce the rework time to x% of the development time (level 4)

● to control the introduction of a new technology (all levels)

● to improve productivity while keeping maintenance quality (level 3)

● to improve customer satisfaction (level 3)

You will find further examples of goals in Appendix 2.

Using the SEI model

The SEI Capability Assessment can be used to identify improvement goals. For each level of maturity in the SEI model there are key activities which must be in place. The SEI questionnaire identifies if these activities are present and properly integrated into the development process. The SEI assessment will identify those activities in your organization that are weak or lacking and stop you achieving a high level of maturity.

Many companies using the SEI Capability Maturity Model to assess their software environment also aim to raise their level in the maturity scale. The SEI model makes general recommendations about procedures which should be implemented to reach the next level. Primary goals for metrication usually match the general recommendations for reaching the next level. Indeed, the levels are designed so that a step up the scale represents a measure of improvement that is achievable over a reasonable period. Here are some recommendations given by SEI on the actions needed to raise maturity level.

Organizations at level 1 (INITIAL)

To improve to level 2, basic project controls must be instituted. The most important are:

- *Project management*: develop plans, determine schedules, evaluate resources, write specifications for development.

- *Management overview*: review and approval of all major plans prior to official commitment, carry out periodic project status review.

- *Quality assurance*: independently validate and verify software development.

- *Change control*: manage and introduce changes in an orderly way.

Organizations at level 2 (REPEATABLE)

To improve to level 3, the development process must be defined. The key actions are:

- *Process group*: establish a group with responsibility for defining the process, identify technology needs, periodically review process status.

- *Process architecture*: establish the development life cycle, technical and managerial tasks and milestones.

- *Process technology*: introduce a family of software engineering methods and technologies, consider prototyping, consider adopting new implementation languages.

Organizations at level 3 (DEFINED)

To improve to level 4, process measurement must be instituted. The most important steps are:

- *Detailed process metrics*: establish a basic set of process measurements to identify costs and benefits of each major process task (e.g. cost and yield of error detection and correction methods).

- *Process database*: establish and maintain a database of process metrics for data obtained from, and available to, all projects.

- *Provide resources*: provide resources to collect, verify, enter and maintain data in the database and advise on analysis methods and interpretation.

- *Quality management*: an independent quality assurance group to track each project against its quality plan and targets, and alert management to deviations in the process.

Organizations at level 4 (MANAGED)

To improve to level 5 (OPTIMIZED), the two fundamental requirements are:

- *Automatic data collection*: automatic data collection reduces problems associated with manual data collection such as error omission and inaccuracy. Also some data cannot be gathered by hand.

- *Process tuning*: use process data both to analyse and modify the process to prevent problems and improve efficiency.

Table 3.2 is a more detailed example that shows how different primary goals can be chosen depending on process capability maturity, initiator and time-scale.

Table 3.2 How goal selection is affected by maturity, initiation and time-scale.

	INITIATOR is	
Assessment result	**Department manager**	**Project manager**
SEI level 1 Low understanding of software development	Short term: to control costs and plans.	Short term: to set up better project control.
	Medium term: to model the software process.	Medium term: to use methods and tools for requirements and design.

Table 3.2 How goal selection is affected by maturity, initiation and time-scale.　　　(cont.)

	INITIATOR is	
Assessment result	**Department manager**	**Project manager**
SEI level 2 Software process is controlled	Short term: to gain a better understanding of project costs.	Short term: provide information on the degree of compliance to project standards and procedures.
	Medium term: to gain a better understanding of project software quality.	Medium term: to provide a greater insight into the calibration of COCOMO for project use.

Identifying other participants

When the primary goals have been selected, it is necessary to identify the other participants and their responsibilities in the
measurement programme. The following questions have to be
answered:

- Who writes the measurement plan?

- Who is the metrics promoter?

- Is an external consultant needed?

- Who else within the organization is involved?

- For which entities are they responsible?

- What are their areas of particular expertise and interests?

- What is the time-scale available for the measurement plan?

- What are the review milestones?

- What is the meetings schedule?

You should nominate a single individual responsible for the measurement plan. He or she will be either internal or external to the
company or group carrying out the measurement. It is extremely
useful to chart the organizational links between people who have
been identified as participants in the measurement activity and
users of its results, and to indicate clearly their respective roles (see
Figure 3.3).

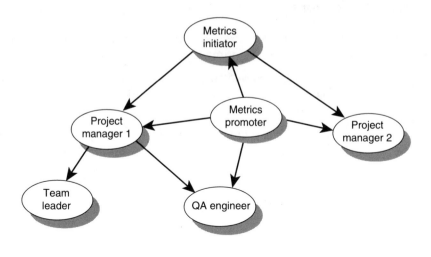

Figure 3.3 A simple organizational chart for participants in the measurement programme.

Example: Step 2 for the Guinea Pig Project

The results from the SEI assessment had shown that there was a need for knowledge goals rather than improvement. This meant that the measurement programme needed to measure the existing level of quality so that an improvement in quality could subsequently be measured. The target of setting about improving the quality by reorganizing the project would need to be postponed until the existing quality could be measured. In parallel with this the development process would be defined and checked against actual practice within the project.

The top-level goal for the Guinea Pig Project was identified as:

Main Goal

To gain better understanding of product quality

The time-scale set to achieve this was a year. It would cover about four deliveries to the customer and would allow the Metrics Promoter to get a large enough set of data to start to identify trends in the data.

Recommendations

Here are some recommendations from the **ami** validation projects for dealing with the primary goals definition:

- *Don't be over-ambitious.* Use fewer but more focused goals. Don't push projects too hard: work within their current maturity limits.

- *Consolidate your foundations first.* Don't try to set primary goals too far above your present understanding and maturity level. It causes disappointment when analysing the benefits of measurement. A control type primary goal must come before an improvement type primary goal.

- *Define your time-scales.* Avoid long-term and general goals especially if this is your first use of the **ami** method.

Step 3: Validating primary goals

3

Validate your primary goals to ensure

- consistency between goals and your assessment conclusions

- consistency between selected goals and time-scales

- consistency between goals and measurement budget

You may be tempted to skimp this task but it is a false economy. A number of **ami** validation projects omitted the validation step and ended up in trouble requiring them to revise their goals while they were collecting the metrics.

The following are watchpoints for checking goals:

(1) High-level goals must be appropriate for your maturity level and be consistent with your company strategy. For example, if your company's global strategy is currently to change the technology and the image of the company given to the customers, a productivity-oriented high-level goal is not appropriate. The Metrics Initiator is the person who has the job of resolving contradictions between goals.

(2) There should not be too many high-level goals. If there are, this could mean collecting a large number of metrics and hence require a disproportionately large amount of effort. Two to three high-level goals will probably be adequate. Also with

a large number of high-level goals there is an increased chance that there will be contradictions. The **ami** validation projects, however, did discover that in selecting high-level goals some turned out to be sub-goals of the others.

For each goal you need to check the following.

- *Relevance*: is the focus and content of the goals appropriate for the decisions that need to be made?

- *Level of detail*: is the level of coverage and detail of the environment appropriate and in accord with the participants' responsibilities?

- *Feasibility*: are the goals over-ambitious compared to the maturity level or the measurement budget?

- *Time-scale*: are the goals short-term, medium-term or long-term?

The Metrics Initiator and the promoter have to resolve the inconsistencies and contradictions. Setting priorities should help. We would recommend that priority should be given to the level of experience in measurement and of your present understanding of the environment and external constraints.

Measuring the effectiveness of the **ami** method

We have already pointed out in Chapter 2 that the **ami** method should be evaluated and the benefits gained identified. Some indicators to do this were also identified there. It is during the validation step that you should consider which of these indicators you want to use, in order to ensure consistency between them and the primary goals.

For example, if the primary goal belongs to the 'knowledge' class, the corresponding indicators need to measure the progress of the knowledge or control achieved. If, on the other hand, it is an 'achievement' goal, indicators need to demonstrate the extent of the improvement.

The Metrics Promoter is the one who is likely to be given this task and will need to ensure that the necessary mechanisms are included to collect the information and that the metrics proposed will provide a good measure for the success of the measurement programme. This activity might be considered as a self-measurement initiative.

Example: Step 3 for the Guinea Pig Project

The goals were assessed by the Metrics Promoter. They were in line with the assessment level since the improvement goal has been changed to a knowledge goal. The time-scale is consistent with the ambition of the goal and would provide a reasonable target to achieve.

Making it easy: setting expectations

Other factors are important too. If the benefits of the metrication programme are expected too early within the time schedule, the results might be disappointing. General rules and practices are as follows:

- With control and knowledge goals, preliminary results can be expected to be achieved after six months and can be refined later.

- With improvement goals, do not expect validated results in less than a year.

Recommendations

- *Don't skip the validation step.*
  - Check goals against implicit project goals and ongoing improvement actions to avoid distracting projects with incompatible goals.
  - Solve contradictions or explain them carefully.

- *Distribute the preliminary results widely.*
  - Don't forget to maintain the motivation of the participants by distributing the validated primary goals with their justification.
  - Take care with psychological aspects.

- *Consider budget.*
  - Verify that allocated budget and primary goals are consistent.
  - If not decide either to modify your budget or modify your primary goals.

Deriving Metrics

The purpose of this activity is to break down the primary goals into more manageable sub-goals, and to clarify the measurement objectives of all the main participants in the measurement process.

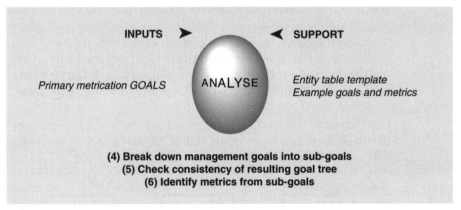

INPUTS ➤ ◄ SUPPORT

Primary metrication GOALS ANALYSE Entity table template
Example goals and metrics

(4) Break down management goals into sub-goals
(5) Check consistency of resulting goal tree
(6) Identify metrics from sub-goals

ami steps 4–6

Chapter 4

Fast track

Plan of action

A small working group analyses the primary goals. The group should consist of a metrics promoter and the managers and engineers who are affected by the goals.

Each primary goal is analysed and broken down into sub-goals to create a goal tree. There is also a table of questions that document the thinking process of how each branch was derived. The final questions (at the end of each branch) are a specification for the metrics.

One of the main objectives of the analysis is to set goals that correspond to domains of responsibility and to the decision-making activity of teams or individuals. The measurement data that is collected will then support decision making and goal achievement. The goal tree is used later when the measurement data is exploited.

A second objective is to achieve greater precision in the primary goals. A goal tree can be used to trace back from customer quality requirements to processes that affect that quality. It can be used to trace complex entities back to constituent entities and attributes.

Once created, the goal tree (Figure 4.1) is checked for consistency of sub-goals with primary goals and of goals with decision making.

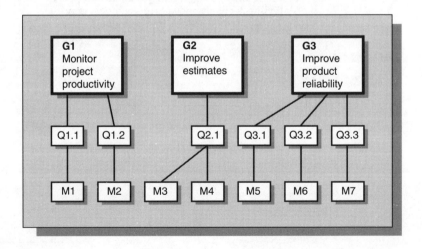

Figure 4.1 Goal tree.

Example: primary goal analysis

The result of the analysis activity can be illustrated with an example. We continue with the first three primary goals presented in Chapter 3, Fast track, which were derived from the primary goal 'Improve customer satisfaction'.

G1 Monitor project productivity

Productivity is defined in terms of the number of units of resource required to produce a unit of product; for example, lines of code per man day. Units of output have to be defined according to the appropriate output category, for example, code size measures, function points measures, documentation size measures, etc. Units of input include common effort measures (e.g. man-months).

There are other aspects of productivity that you might take into account in analysing goals. You might want to look at how your procedures are affecting productivity. For example, is reuse of existing code or designs being used as much as it could, or, are your designs taking full advantage of commercial off-the-shelf packages?

To identify the sub-goals of goal G1, it will help to ask some additional questions about how the different participants might see advantages in increased productivity from the point of view of the product and the resources used:

● what is of value to the customer? – fewer errors?

● what is of value to your organization? – delivery on schedule?

● what will reduce resource usage? – reuse of code?

These result in a set of metrics, for example:

● project delivered lines of source code (SLOC) /man-month

● percentage of components reused

● percentage of rework effort

G2 Improve estimates

Your questions are likely to be about the accuracy of your budget and schedule estimates. Some possible metrics are:

● difference between estimates and actuals

● correlation between estimates and actuals

G3 Improve product reliability

Users of this goal typically have found they need to know how many errors there are, their location, their type, and how much and how rigorous was the testing. Some possible metrics are:

- error location

- error category

- percentage test coverage

- test effort man hours

- inspection effort man hours

This example illustrates some important features of goal-oriented measurement. Different goals affect different people. Project productivity mainly concerns the project manager, while product reliability is the concern of the quality assurance engineer. Conversely, global long-term monitoring of results from all the organization's projects are of interest to higher-level management.

The goals, questions and sub-goals form a tree. Metrics are linked to goals. Metrics for higher-level goals tend to be aggregates of metrics at the lower level. The goal tree provides the framework for your measurement programme. Within it you can plan the detail of your programme, identify resources and responsibilities, and plan how the analysis of the results will be carried out.

Step 4: From goals to sub-goals

The **ami** approach to goal-driven derivation of metrics is adapted from the Goal–Question–Metric (GQM) method. GQM was devised by Victor Basili at the University of Maryland in 1985 and further refined during his work with the NASA Goddard Space Center (see Basili (1988) for more details). The reasons for selecting this method are its flexibility and adaptability to any type of organization and metrication objective, it is based on good sense and is well founded. The method has been adapted to the **ami** approach.

A complex goal will need to be divided into sub-goals before you can identify metrics for it. The analysis of primary goals is achieved either by a series of interviews conducted by a metrics promoter, or by a simple analysis carried out by each person affected by the goals and coordinated via a working group. In both cases, a top-down step-by-step analysis is necessary. This top-down approach is needed to translate the primary goals into more pragmatic (that is, less global and strategic) sub-goals related to the activities processed by each participant.

For example, for the goal *'to gain a better understanding of project costs'* you will need to identify all those things related to project costs and which have an impact on them such as budgets, project plans and requirements. You should discuss the sub-goals with the participants who have control over these or can have an influence on them. For the example these might be:

- customers who affect costs by requesting changes,

- project managers who provide and control resources (people, computers, etc.),

- team leaders and engineers in the project who help make the technical decisions and carry out the work.

Analysing the goals you will involve participants who have different roles within your organization. They will have different information needs, viewpoints and objectives. They will range from the broad strategic business to detail technical. Each will have different responsibilities and spheres of influence and will therefore have a different perspective. This consequently leads to different formulations of the primary goals. To help ensure that you are thorough we recommend that in your discussions with the participants you systematically consider the products and processes for which they have responsibility.

You will find that as you refine the sub-goals to lower levels you will get into more and more detail and, in the process, go down to lower levels of the company reporting structure. However, you should not blindly follow the company reporting structure; it does not always reflect how the work is actually structured. In doing the analysis you must bear in mind the way the work is broken into processes and tasks.

Having identified the products and processes that are associated with the goal, you should then go on to consider with the participants responsible for each of the products and processes, how they affect the achievement of the goal. In clarifying the views and objectives of the participants in relation to the goals you will produce a set of questions. This makes it easier for you to select the most appropriate sub-goals. For example, in taking improvement of quality as a goal you will need to establish what you understand by quality, what contributes or degrades the quality of your product, the ways in which you want to improve quality, and what you need to know to identify where improvements can be made. The answers to these questions are used to formulate the questions that will lead to the formulation of the next level goal. In the example, we may have decided that the quality of the requirement specification has a strong effect on product quality. A sub-goal would then be to improve the quality of requirement specifications.

The questions represent the participant's viewpoint of the primary goals selected by the initiator. Questions help each group to clarify how they are affected by the primary goal according to:

- the products under their responsibility and more particularly the characteristics of those products (that is, readability of a document, complexity of a piece of code),

- the processes in which they are involved and/or are controlling,

- the resources they are managing.

In other words, questions are related to the sorts of decisions the participants need to take concerning products, processes and resources in relation to the primary goal. The type of decision is determined by the role of the decision maker within the project, department or company. For example, a project manager is responsible for project planning but it may not be his responsibility to engage new staff. This is the job of the department manager.

The goal tree

The results of this analysis will be a goal tree for each primary goal. A goal tree is a hierarchy of goals and sub-goals starting with a primary goal at the top. Each goal and sub-goal has a list of questions associated with it that lead to the related sub-goals. The exceptions are the bottom-most sub-goals which will not have questions associated with them just yet. These will be supplied in Step 6 when we derive the metrics.

It is useful to note, for each sub-goal, the names of the participants who have an interest in the sub-goal and helped in its analysis, plus the entities which were associated with the sub-goal. This information will be valuable when formulating the metrics in Step 6 and analysing the results in Steps 10 to 12.

Using your maturity level to determine goals

The SEI capability maturity model identifies a number of key processes which must be in place in a company at a given level of maturity. This also provides a way of identifying the areas that need to be addressed in identifying goals. The SEI model recommends that you first focus on getting your project management right and then on improving your development processes. Table 4.1 summarizes these areas.

Table 4.1 Example goals to match maturity level.

Level	Primary goal	Sub-goal
5: Optimized	Continuous process improvement	Defect prevention Technology innovation Process change managemen
4: Managed	Product and process quality	Process measurement and analysis Quality management
3: Defined	Quality and productivity via engineering process	Organization process focus Organization process definition Peer reviews Training programme Inter-group coordination Software product engineering Integrated software management
2: Repeatable	Quality and productivity via project management	S/w project planning S/w project tracking S/w subcontract management S/w quality assurance S/w configuration management Requirements management

You will notice that the table does not include level 1. This is the lowest level and is characterized by not having enough of the key processes to make level 2. To move up a level you will need to implement those processes identified as key for the next level. However, remember that to achieve the next level you must have all the key processes in place for all the lower levels. The table indicates that

Table 4.2 Potential goals and sub-goals for a level 1 company.

Primary goals	Sub-goal	Typical metrics
Understand the effectiveness of project management	Effectiveness of planning	Actual and estimated costs
	Effectiveness of progress monitoring	No. of plan updates
	Effectiveness of sub-contracting	Cost and schedules of sub-contracts
	Effectiveness of quality assurance	No. of audits No. of deficiencies Time to clear deficiencies
	Effectiveness of configuration management	No. of errors caused by defective configuration management No. of modules under configuration management
	Effectiveness of requirements management	No. of requirements changes per phase

companies at level 1 should concentrate on establishing effective project management to get to level 2. A list of potential goals and sub-goals suitable for a level 1 company is given in Table 4.2.

Example: Step 4 for the Guinea Pig Project

In the Guinea Pig Project the Metrics Promoter identified the goals with the metrics initiator who in this case was the Project Manager. The first task was to identify the Products and Processes that the Project Manager controlled. These are summarized in Table 4.3 in relation to the goal of understanding product quality. This example has been simplified to make it easier to follow. The Project Manager's interest was in obtaining a measure of the quality of the product he delivered to the customer and to determine if some parts of the software are more difficult to get right than others. He was also interested in how the separate processes affect the quality of the product.

Table 4.3 Entities managed by the Project Manager, and related questions.

Entities	Questions
Products:	
System	Q1. How does the quality vary through the different modules of the software?
	Q2. What is the quality of the product delivered to the customer?
Processes:	
Development	Q3. How do the different processes of the development process affect the quality of the software?

Sub-goals from Project Manager Viewpoint

SG1. To understand how the different parts of the software affect quality. (Q1)

SG2. To gain a measure of the quality of the delivered software. (Q2)

SG3. To understand how different parts of the development process affect quality. (Q3)

The Metrics Promoter next talked to the team leaders and project quality engineer. The resulting entities and questions are given in Table 4.4. You should note in order to make a simple example we are analysing goals further than is strictly necessary. It would have been possible to identify the metrics after identifying these questions.

To simplify the example further we have only considered a few aspects of quality: namely, error levels in the delivered code and the efficiency of the development process at eliminating errors before delivery to the customer. In practice there may be more quality factors that should be considered. It was part of the Metrics Promoter's responsibility to determine what the initiator and participants understand by quality and what they saw as key factors of quality in their environment. The Metrics Promoter also talked to customers to discover what they felt were the key factors in quality.

Table 4.4 Entities managed by development team leaders related to SG3.

Entities	Questions
Products:	
Requirement specification	Q3.1 What is the quality of the requirement spec.?
Design specification	Q3.2 What is the quality of the design spec.?
Module code	Q3.3 What is the quality of the module code?
Test plan	Q3.4 What is the quality of the module test plan?
Processes:	
Requirements analysis	Q3.5 How effective is requirements analysis at detecting errors?
Design and code	Q3.6 How effective is the design and code process at detecting errors?
Module test	Q3.7 How effective is the module test at detecting errors?

The project now had a list of the relevant products and processes. Since they were focusing on errors they needed to look at these in relation to how they might cause errors and how effective they are at detecting and eliminating errors; in other words, how they contribute to the quality of the final product. The questions that were posed for each item in the table were targeted at getting this insight. They looked at the distribution of error reports over the different processes. In looking at the error reports, they realized that it was important to decide whether to include those generated internally to the project as well as those from the customer. Since they wanted to consider the efficiency of their processes at detecting errors, they elected to include internally generated error reports and include comments from design reviews.

You will notice that the focus is to try to identify where the errors were caused and how well the processes can detect errors. The Development Team Leaders identified that the quality of the delivered product is related to the quality of the intermediate products, namely requirement specification, design specification, module code, and so on.

From this list of questions they formulate the following sub-goals.

Sub-goals from Development Team Leader viewpoint

SG3.1 To determine the quality of the intermediate products.

(Q3.1, Q3.2, Q3.3, Q3.4)

SG3.2 To determine how effective processes are at detecting errors.

(Q3.5, Q3.6, Q3.7)

Making it easy: use entities

To help focus the analysis it helps to identify the entities associated with a particular goal. In the present context we will define an entity as:

- **Entity** Any aspect of the process, business activity or project plan connected to a measurement programme participant (e.g. project planning, design document);

- **Attribute** Any characteristic or property of an entity.

Entities are typically products, processes or resources. In general, metrics measure the attributes of entities.

With goals at high strategic levels it can be difficult to identify suitable entities. For example, a goal like *'to increase market penetration of a particular product'*. In such cases you must do without the help of entities. However, as your analysis proceeds to greater detail, you will begin to identify suitable entities for the sub-goals.

If your company or department uses a clearly defined and documented development process, the entities will be easily identified. If not, current practices should be analysed to identify the entities.

Participants can be associated with particular types of entities they control. This can also help divide participants into groups.

When doing Step 4, it is a good idea to draw a set of tables similar to those shown in the example project. A table should be produced for each goal and participant. Committing them to paper can help make your thinking more precise as well as providing a record.

Listing entities creates a template for asking questions. To create this list of entities, the resources, processes (or tasks) and products that make up a project must be identified. The project might be using a software development standard or an in-house quality manual. Many of the entities will be defined in these documents. The standard or manual can be used as an input for this step. Take care to list all the entities that exist in practice (and only these) even if this is not quite what is in the standard.

This step is simply repeated for each organizational level from the initiator downwards until the detailed work processes are reached where primitive data can be collected. Asking questions helps the participants to see how to break down the goal into sub-goals and helps them to clarify and understand the primary goals. The entities for which the participants are responsible will act as a focus for your questions.

Recommendations

Here are some recommendations from the **ami** validation projects about goal tree decomposition:

- *Keep it simple.* If you have only just started your metrication programme, don't try to draw too complex a goal tree. One or two primary goals and two levels of breakdown should suffice. This will allow you to build up your experience and optimize your procedures.

- *Consolidate your foundations first.* Ensure that primary goals and goal trees are consistent with your maturity level and with available resources.

- *Make use of your codes of practice.* Look at your company life-cycle standards to analyse entities and clearly identify which managers make the decisions.

- *Use the examples in Appendix 2.* Compare your sub-goals with those in Appendix 2. They may give you ideas on how to improve yours.

Step 5 : Verifying the goal tree

The goal tree that results from analysis of the primary goal should be verified. You should check for the following:

- the global balance of the tree,

- the internal consistency of the tree and the absence of contradiction between goals and sub-goals,

- the external consistency of the tree.

The **global balance** of the tree is very simply the uniformity of detail in each branch. The detail of the goal tree usually indicates the level of understanding that the project has already achieved. The more branches there are, the more extensive the data collection will be. In checking the balance you need to ask the following questions:

- Are the branches broken down similarly?

- If not, what is the reason for the imbalance?

- Is the breakdown consistent with the responsibility level of the participants?

- Are the participants at each level really responsible for the entities they have identified?

- Are the entities and participants consistent with the identified goals?

- If the participants are not responsible for the entities, will they have access to the information?

- Are the communications channels clearly defined?

Internal consistency is checked between levels. The following questions will need to be asked:

- Are sub-goals a real expression of the next goal up the tree?

- Is there any other viewpoint for the goal?

- Do sub-goals belong to the same class as the goal?

- Are there contradictions between sub-goals of different branches?

External consistency is the validation of the relevance of the goal tree to primary goals. It should verify that the refinement of primary goals has not resulted in contradictions.

If an inconsistency or a contradiction is discovered, you must resolve the problem. The approaches that you could consider to resolve problems are:

- Rework the primary goal starting from the validated results of the previous **ami** step.

- Rework the specific branch of the tree causing the problem with the relevant participants.

- Accept the contradiction since it concerns different participants and work it out later when the metrics are available.

- Accept the contradiction because it is the only inconsistency in the development process. The measurement initiative could help to resolve it.

Contradictions might be due to unstated goals, as in the following example.

Suppose your primary goals are to 'improve development productivity' and 'decrease time to market', but you have no goal relating to quality. You can achieve both these primary goals by reducing the time and effort given to testing. This would almost certainly lead to a decrease in the effort required to produce lines of code, and a shorter development schedule. However, it would probably lead to a poorer quality product and increased support costs. In such a case, the measurement programme would indicate that the required improvement was happening because the stated goals were being achieved.

Example: Step 5 for the Guinea Pig Project

In this example we will go through some of the checks identified in the description of this step and show how they were checked on the Guinea Pig Project.

Internal and external consistency

Are sub-goals a real expression of the next goal up the tree? The Metrics Promoter examined the arguments used to derive the metrics and ensured that they were logical and provided a complete answer to the requirements of the higher-level goal. For example, consider sub-goal 3.2 from the Development Team Leaders: '*To determine how effective processes are at detecting errors*' and its relation to the main goal '*To gain a better understanding of product quality*'. The sub-goal identifies error levels as an important aspect of quality. The Metrics Promoter verified that this was the relevant aspect of quality and that it was also the customers' view. The other aspect the Metrics Promoter checked was whether the two sub-goals give a sufficiently complete picture to gain the understanding needed.

Are there any other viewpoints? The Metrics Promoter checked the list of potential participants to ensure that no one relevant had been omitted. He also checked with the Project Manager whether anyone further needed to be consulted.

Recommendations

- *Don't skip the validation step.* Rectifying errors discovered later can be expensive and demotivating.

- *Review your sub-goals with all participants.* Give all the participants a chance to comment on the sub-goals; they could well help improve them.

Step 6: From sub-goals to metrics

Once you have a verified goal tree, the next step is to derive the metrics to match the sub-goals. Metrics derivation starts from the bottom of the goal tree. The object in analysing the goals into sub-goals is to make this step easier. Thus the bottom level corresponds to your elementary work processes. The entities that are associated with the bottom-level sub-goals should be tangible and have attributes that are measurable. The task is thus one of identifying the appropriate measurable attributes that can be collected. Table 4.5 shows some examples of entities and attributes that you are likely to encounter in your projects.

Table 4.5 Example entities and attributes.

Entity	Attribute
Software product	Size, reliability, etc.
Testing process	Duration, effectiveness, etc.
Accommodation	Area, comfort, etc.

The questioning process is used to identify metrics in the same way as Step 4. A metric will be an attribute of an entity. The entity will be the one the question is being asked about.

Subjective and objective metrics

At this stage of the **ami** method, we must introduce subjective and objective metrics. Objective metrics are easily quantified and generally correspond to the attributes of entities. Whenever possible, it is recommended that objective metrics are used.

Subjective metrics are qualitative. They are generally explanations that qualify the context of the project. They are expressed on scales such as 'very bad, bad, medium, good, very good' and have no absolute value. Human factors and quality of documentation are examples of subjective metrics. It is often useful to have some subjective metrics and qualitative information to help interpret objective metrics.

Completing the goal tree

When metrics have been derived at the lowest level, the goal tree must be used from bottom to top. Metrics associated with the sub-goals of a particular goal are generally combined to derive new metrics associated with this higher-level goal. New questions may be needed to give precise quantification of goals. A simple example is the quality of the software defined as the ratio of the number of errors found by the test team to the number of lines developed by the software team.

At the end of this step you should have a goal tree with metrics associated for all goals and sub-goals. An extensive example of a goal tree including metrics is given in Appendix 2 for a wide range of goals. This table should help you to decide which goals you should go for.

Example: Step 6 for the Guinea Pig Project

To illustrate this aspect of the **ami** method we will make use of the questions from the Development Team Leaders used in the sub-goal derivation. You may have noticed that this set of questions could lead directly to metrics without going via sub-goals. We will start from the set of questions given in Table 4.4. You should note that in a real case these questions could be merged with questions from other viewpoints to give a simpler, more concise goal tree.

The set of metrics which might be derived from these questions are summarized below.

Metrics derived from Team Leader questions associated with SG3

M3.1 Customer queries traceable to a problem in the Requirements Specification.

M3.2 Customer queries traceable to a problem in the Design Specification.

M3.3 Customer queries traceable to a problem in the module code.

M3.4 Customer queries traceable to a problem in the module test plan.

M3.5 Number of errors detected during requirements analysis.

M3.6 Number of errors detected in design and code review process.

M3.7 Number of errors detected in module test.

The next part of this task is to go back up the tree identifying the metrics associated with the questions and their related sub-goals. Starting with the questions above you will be able to see how this is done. The metric associated with Q3.1, M3.1, is a count on the number of customer errors associated with requirements analysis. This was consolidated with the metric data associated with Q3.2, Q3.3, and Q3.4 to give a picture of the distribution of customer errors over the processes. This combined metric provides information to sub-goals 3 *to understand better how different parts of the development process affect quality.* This in turn feeds into question Q2 of the main goal. This is summarized below.

Metrics supporting SG3

M1: No. of customer queries attributable to each process.

(Q3.1, Q3.2, Q3.3, Q3.4)

M2: No. of errors detected during each process.

(Q3.5, Q3.6, Q3.7)

M3: No. of changes to intermediate products due to queries.

(Q3.1, Q3.2, Q3.3, Q3.4)

When identifying metrics it was necessary to think through the definition of what needed to be included in the collection of data. In the case of the number of error counts they needed to think carefully about whether to include all comments raised from design reviews and to check carefully whether there were any other sources of error reports which were not recorded.

Making it easy: use existing know how

Use well-tried metrics. The example metrics given in Appendix 3 are based on experience. The list is based on evidence from the ESPRIT projects MUSE, REQUEST and SPEM. Where possible, you should select and build upon the objective metrics given there. Many code and design metrics can be extracted with the aid of software tools. Analysis of the results supported the view that only a few metrics are useful and that many complex metrics offer no advantage over those which are comparatively simple to collect.

Use qualitative and quantitative metrics. It must be emphasized again that the selected objective metrics must be complemented by subjective metrics so as to explain the context.

Recommendations

Here are some recommendations from experience of using the **ami** method. Although the following recommendations may appear to be aimed at first time users, we would stress that they can be used as a check list by those who have already started measurement but are new to goal-oriented measurement:

- *Think it through yourself.* Try to define your own goal tree and metrics rather than using one from another company. Use metrics that can be understood by all the participants and involve them in the validation process.

- *Keep it simple.* Start with simple and general usable metrics. Avoid poor subjective quality metrics.

- *Exploit existing information.* Most organizations already collect useful data such as cost data and effort. Exploiting these can be a cost-effective way of starting off.

- *Write it down.* Be aware of the relevance and importance of the questions in the goal breakdown and in the metrics derivation. They must be written down.

- *Communicate.* Use metrics that can be understood by all the participants and involve them.

Implementing a
Measurement Plan

In this chapter we look at how to write a measurement plan, how to implement the plan and then how to go about collecting the primitive data from which the metrics are derived.

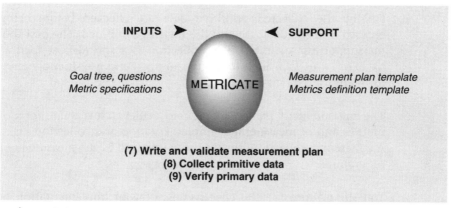

INPUTS ▶   **◀ SUPPORT**

Goal tree, questions   *Measurement plan template*
Metric specifications   *Metrics definition template*

METRICATE

(7) Write and validate measurement plan
(8) Collect primitive data
(9) Verify primary data

ami steps 7–9

Chapter 5

Fast track

Plan of action

The results from the activities described in Chapters 3 and 4 are the starting point for writing the project's measurement plan. The plan is written by the metrics promoter and validated by those involved in the definition and derivation of goals.

From the metric's specification a complete definition of the metric and the analysis and collection procedures are produced. A metrics template is used to support this process.

The implementation tasks are then prepared. Collection forms and simple tools are produced. The forms should be clearly laid out with boxes for identifying the measured entities and background information such as date and collector's name. Tools for data collection should be used whenever possible. Simple counting tools can often be developed in-house.

Finally, the collected primitive data are checked before being entered into the database and the metrics computed. The best tool for supporting an initial data collection is a spreadsheet such as Excel or Lotus 123. Such tools give an open and user-friendly environment for data management.

The measurement plan helps you to achieve clear definitions of metrics and of measurement implementation and collection tasks. A coherent approach motivates those involved in the measurement programme.

You should measure the effectiveness of your implementation of the plan. The plan can be incorporated into project or department plans and be subjected to the same review procedures. Regular feedback of metrics for analysis will help validate and further motivate those involved. A consolidated measurement report presented to management at regular intervals, say, every three months, helps to keep higher management involved.

Example: writing a measurement plan

A measurement plan template has been used by members of the **ami** consortium. It is a good example of what a plan should contain, and we recommend that you use it as well. The document is structured as follows:

- *Part 1: Objectives of the measurement plan*
  In this part, the context, assessment conclusions, goals and questions are detailed. There is a summary of the results of the work carried out in Steps 1 to 6 of the **ami** method. This information is crucial for correct metrics definition and exploitation of measurement data.

- *Part 2: Metrics Definitions*
  A precise definition and analysis procedure is given for each metric. It should include the question which specified it and the goal to which it is linked in the goal tree; those who analyse the metric and will receive the results are identified; how and when the measurement data is to be presented is stated. Each metric is made up of one or more primitive metrics, and these should be clearly identified. The precise collection procedure should be defined. Examples of metrics definitions can be found in Appendix 3.

- *Part 3: Responsibilities and time-scales*
  All major responsibilities and milestones should appear in this section. In some cases those responsible for different activities will be able to draw up their own plans. If this is so, these later activities need not be included here.

- *Part 4: References*
  Relevant references and support material are listed.

- *Part 5: Logbook for measurement activities*
  A logbook kept during the project helps in the monitoring activity and in the analysis of the metrics. The contents and entry types are defined in this section.

The following sections include a more detailed description of the template.

Step 7: The measurement plan

This document is one of the first fruits of your investment in software measurement. In addition to being a plan for the collection of data, it is a record of your software development environment, your development process, the strengths and weaknesses of the environment and process, and a standard for communication between the participants in your metrication programme. An outline contents of the measurement plan is given in the Fast track section of this chapter. We will now go into more detail of the content of the plan.

This measurement plan template was extensively used by the **ami** consortium's 19 validation projects. Feedback from these projects has given us confidence that it is a good structure for the plan. We would recommend that if you do not follow this exact structure you at least review the sorts of contents that are included in the template below for inclusion in your plans.

In producing the plan you should have the following objectives in mind:

- To formalize the results of discussions about the measurement programme.

- To formalize the organizational framework so that everyone involved is aware of what they must do.

- To serve as an introduction for newcomers to the measurement programme.

- To maintain motivation and provide background for the programme's participants.

The measurement plan constitutes the reference document for your measurement programme and a moral contract between initiator, metrics promoter and participants. We would recommend that it should be accepted and agreed by them all before you start to collect data.

Contents of the measurement plan

The following detailed contents list for a measurement plan will give you a good idea of what you will want to include in your plans.

Part 1: Objectives of the measurement plan

Introduction
A general section that describes the context of the measurement programme, the main characteristics of the company (or project), software development strategies employed, and the type of project involved. The value of this section will be increased if the general principles and motivation for the metrication programme are

explained. It could include, for example, the benefits found in other organizations from using metrics, technology transfer from other disciplines, and references to further background reading.

Assessment

The approach used to assess the environment is described in this section together with the results of the assessment. A summary of the work carried out in Steps 1 to 3 should be included with a summary of the conclusions. It should indicate the areas in which improvements will be sought. It should prepare the ground for the goal section that follows it. This information is important background for the proper understanding of the metric definitions and for the exploitation of measurement data.

Goal tree

The list of the primary goals and their justification should be provided in this section. It is important to include the table of entities (if these have been produced) and the questions that were used during the decomposition of the goals into sub-goals. You should explain how the goals, sub-goals and questions are logically related so that the reader will understand the thinking that has gone into selecting the metrics.

Part 2: Metrics definition

A precise definition and an analysis procedure should be given for each metric. The way a metric is derived from a goal question and is linked to one or more goals should be carefully explained. The collection and the use of each data item should be defined with its frequency of use. The type of plot used to present the metrics should be identified. The details of the metrics definition template are given below in the section of the same name.

Part 3: Responsibilities and time-scales

This section should define the main responsibilities for the measurement programme. It should cover the responsibilities of the initiator, the metrics promoter and the other participants.

The organization of data collection should be laid down and cover planning, budget and schedules. One of the objectives of a measurement programme is to make decisions about when and how to improve. The schedules should include the time at which sufficient information is expected to be available to enable planning decisions to be made. The plan should include the main milestones of the initiative – for example, the start and finish of the **ami** steps and the dates of the measurement plan reviews. The budget should include the effort allocated to the initiative.

Part 4: Referenced documents

The list of references should include the titles and complete references to **ami** material and other sources used on the initiative. It should allow the interested reader to obtain a more detailed background to measurement and access to the details of earlier work in the measurement programme.

Part 5: Logbook for measurement activities

ami advocates the keeping of a logbook to help monitor and analyse the measurement programme, and to act as a central repository of information for the metrics promoter. A format for the logbook should be included in the plan. This can include the type of information to be recorded and when it should be updated. It is essential that the procedure used is simple and practical.

Should it be easier, the measurement plan can be prepared incrementally, with part 1 being prepared first and parts 2, 3 and 4 completed later. The plan should be completed and agreed before Step 8 is started.

Metrics definition template

At first sight it may seem unnecessary to define each metric in detail. However, experience over many years, supported by results from **ami** validation projects, has shown that defining the metrics precisely before you start collection does produce benefits. Good definitions help to achieve the precision and objectivity that are the aim of a measurement programme.

The template is divided into two parts. Part A covers the definition of the metrics which will be presented to the participants for analysis. Part B covers the definition and collection procedures for the primitive metrics which are used to calculate the other metrics. It is possible the primitive metric may also be analysed directly, in which case it should appear in both parts A and B. If there is extensive overlap you might consider merging the entries for parts A and B to make a more compact document.

In the description given below we will need the following definitions:

- A **metric** is a measurable attribute of an entity. For example, for the entity, *project effort* is a measure (i.e. metric) of project size. To be able to calculate this metric you would need to sum all the time-sheet bookings for the project.

- A **primitive metric** is a raw data item that is used to calculate a metric. In the above example the time-sheet bookings are the primitive metrics. A primitive metric is typically a metric that exists in a database but is not interpreted in isolation.

Each metric is made up of one or more collected primitive metrics. Consequentially, each primitive metric has to be clearly identified and the collection procedure defined.

Here is a detailed contents list we suggest you use to define your metrics. Appendix 3 includes some example definitions which follow this format so that you can see how they are used.

Part A: Metric definition and analysis procedure	
A1. Name	Name of the metric and any known synonyms.
A2. Definition	The attributes of the entities that are measured using this metric, how the metric is calculated, and the primitive metrics from which it is calculated.
A3. Goals	List of goals and questions related to the metric. You should include some explanation of why the metric is being collected.
A4. Analysis procedure	How the metric is intended to be used. Preconditions for the interpretation of the metric (e.g. valid ranges of other metrics). Target trends of the metric values. Models or analysis techniques and tools to be used. Implicit assumptions (e.g. of the environment or models). Calibration procedures. Storage.
A5. Responsibilities	Who will collect and aggregate the measurement data, prepare the reports, and analyse the data.
A6. Training required	What training is required for application and interpretation of this metric.

Part B: Primitive definition and collection procedure	
B1. Name	Name of the primitive metric.
B2. Definition	Unambiguous description of the metric in terms of the project's environment.
B3. Collection procedure	Description of the collection procedure. Data collection tool and form to be used. The points in the life cycle when data are collected. The verification procedure to be used. Where the data will be stored, its format and precision.
B4. Responsibilities	Who is responsible for collecting the data. Who is responsible for verifying the data. Who will enter the data into the database. Who has access to modify the data.

For effective measurement, you must have software configuration control in place in your projects. Data collection cannot function properly without it. The entities that you measure are subject to change during the software development process. Where configuration control is not in place, or is weak, a software measurement programme can help to stimulate its proper use.

It is useful to include a summary table of the metrics and the metrics from which it is calculated to act as a quick reference aid.

Validating the plan

Collecting data means putting plans into practice – actually getting measurement installed and working. By this stage you should have the support of all levels of management and staff. The essential compromises and adjustments that are so important to success should have been effected.

Be careful. If you have got this far without considerable modification and rewriting of your plans, you have probably not reviewed them as thoroughly and as critically as necessary. If this is the case, there are likely to be problems waiting to be discovered once the machinery starts turning. Working on moving machinery is not only a very dangerous occupation, but is also not the way to create a good, durable system. We recommend that the plan be verified by someone who was not involved in the metrics derivation and definition task. It should then be validated by those responsible for the goals.

It is important that you check the availability of data before starting collection. In some cases the data, even if it is simple, may not be available unless the internal procedures of the group are changed. You will find it is more efficient to look at the organizational and procedural aspects to discover the difficulties before starting the machinery.

For example, many companies trace effort for software development with time sheets that staff fill in regularly. The range of booking numbers available often do not distinguish between, say, requirement, design or testing activities. If you decide that you want to collect data on the effort used in different activities you may be faced with reorganizing your time-sheet procedures. A simple but less satisfactory alternative might be to ask for a subjective evaluation from each person working on the project.

Other validation checks that you can apply are:

- Check the appropriateness of the metrics:

  - Are the metrics really are under the control of the participants concerned?
  - Is the attribute selected the most pertinent for the sub-goal?
  - Are the metrics easy to collect or to calculate?
  - Is there too high a proportion of subjective metrics?
  - Are the participants happy that the metrics are appropriate for their goals?
  - Do they need more information?
  - Cross-check with metrics on other branches of the goal tree to ensure the metric definitions are consistent and identify common usage of metrics.

- Check the metrics definition against the template above to verify that the definition is complete.

- Make sure the planning is complete.

Example: Step 7 for the Guinea Pig Project

The Metrics Promoter wrote the metrics plan for the Guinea Pig Project and conducted a number of reviews to ensure its quality and that nothing had been forgotten. The following are abstracts from the plan for the Guinea Pig Project.

Part 1: Objectives

Introduction

The Metric Promoter used this section to inform both management and engineers of the aims and scope of the measurement programme. It also set expectations so that managers did not expect too much too soon. It also indicated the benefits to the company, the project and the project personnel.

> 'The management of the Guinea Pig Project are conscious of the need to provide our customer with high quality products. To ensure that we continue to do this and help us improve our performance we are implementing this measurement programme. This will give us an insight into how we are performing and give us clues as to how we can improve.

> 'By getting a better understanding of quality issues we can better control the level of quality incorporated into our products. We can then select a level of quality appropriate for the product and thereby avoid either over-engineering or under-engineering the product.

> 'This programme is intended to be a joint effort by all those on the project and it is not intended that it will measure the performance of any one individual.

> 'The rest of this document will tell you what we intend to do, why we are doing it in the way that we are and what we hope to achieve. This is a joint activity. If anyone sees ways of improving this plan and the activities of the measurement programme the Metrics Promoter will be pleased to hear from you.'

Assessment

For this section the Metric Promoter wanted to explain how they performed the assessment and the main results from the assessment. It was necessary to show what the implications of the maturity level achieved were in terms of the goals that had been set. The Metrics Promoter explained the areas of weakness that had been found and the improvements to the process that were suggested by the SEI maturity model.

Goal tree

In this section the Metrics Promoter explained the goals and metrics that had been selected, the rationale behind the selection and why a particular view of things, like quality measures, had been taken. For example, the following extracts from the Guinea Pig Project measurement plan illustrate this for error level measurement. This explanation would also use the entity/question tables given in the previous chapter.

'We have interpreted quality in terms of error levels in the software delivered to the customer. In our discussions with our customers this was cited as their main concern...

'...From the point of view of error levels, we want to examine which processes gave rise to which sort of errors and how effective our validation procedures are at detecting errors. By relating types of error to detection activities we would be able to find out what sort of procedures are better at detecting what sort of errors. From this we hope to be able to see if we have the right level of validation activity. For example, we might find that design reviews detect certain types of error. These error types are found to be getting through to later processes and we have scope for increasing the number and type of design reviews and hence reducing the number of errors getting through to later processes.'

Part 2: Metrics definition

In this section the Metrics Promoter defined the metrics to be used and the primitive metrics to be collected. An example of each type is included below. You should note that each metric is given a reference number which makes exact identification easier and reduces possible misunderstanding. Also, in precisely defining the metric and the procedure a number of detail problems of interpretation were revealed. For example, in defining the procedure it was identified that the error reports taken into consideration in producing the metric needed to be included to help interpret the metric.

Metric definition

(1)   Metric Name: M6: Error Distribution.

(2)   Definition: This metric shows how the errors reported by the customer are attributed to various processes.

(3)   Goals: This metric is associated with sub-goal 2 – to understand better where errors are introduced.

(4)   Analysis procedure: The project Quality Manager will collect M25 – customer error counts from the appropriate team leaders and produce a table of count against process. The processes that will be considered will be Requirements Analysis, Design and Code, Module Test and Integration Testing. A statement of the error reports covered by the report will be included.

(5)   Responsibilities: The project Quality Manager will be responsible for collecting the counts from the Team Leaders and preparing the metric every month. The Team Leaders will be responsible for collecting M25. The metric will be distributed to the Project Manager and all Team Leaders.

(6)   Training: The Quality Manager will need to be acquainted with the **ami** method. He or she should already understand the project procedures and so should not require further training in this area.

Primitive metric definition

(1)   Name: M25 – customer error report count.

(2)   Definition: This count is made for a particular process. It is a count of the errors reported by customers that are attributable to the process.

(3)   Collection procedure: On receipt of a customer error report, a cause process will be attributed to it. The processes to be considered will be Requirements Analysis, Design and Code, Module Test and Integration Testing. A log of the errors for each process will be kept. At monthly intervals a report of the count will be sent to the project Quality Manager.

(4)   Responsibilities: The project Quality Manager will be responsible for identifying the cause processes. He or she will send these to the responsible Team Leader who is obliged to maintain the log of errors for the processes for which he or she is responsible. The team leaders will at monthly intervals supply a copy of the log to the project Quality Manager.

Part 3: Responsibilities and time-scale

Initiator responsibilities

The Project Managers will be responsible for the initiator role. Their responsibilities will include the provision and administration of the budget for the programme. They will ensure that the responsible people are properly tasked to collect the metrics. They will periodically review the progress of the programme and initiate a modification of the programme in consultation with the Metrics Promoter.

Making it easy: carry out a dry run

A 'dry run' of the collection procedures defined in the measurement plan could be performed to discover any bottlenecks or difficulties. Most of the validation projects that have conducted a 'dry run' reported they needed to make modifications to their measurement plan.

Recommendations

When writing the plan, the following guidelines will help you to develop efficient procedures:

- Check that data collection is integrated into the development process, for example, as part of the configuration, quality or management system.

- Data collection should be automated whenever possible.

- Data that cannot be collected automatically should be collected at the time (i.e. not based on memory) and verified immediately.

- A central collection point should be identified.

- Someone should be available for trouble-shooting in the early days of data collection.

- The time-scale between data collection and data analysis should be kept to a minimum.

- Adequate training in data collection procedures and the use of software metrics should be provided.

- Quick analysis facilities should be available.

- People should be made aware of the plans and procedures and of their responsibilities.

- Finally, never underestimate the problem of motivating people to keep accurate records.

Step 8: Collecting the data

Collecting data is an activity which will be carried out almost continuously during your measurement programme and is likely to involve a large number of people. Here are some ways in which data collection can be made more efficient.

Whichever procedure you put into place, it makes sense after a settling-in period to review regularly how well data collection is proceeding. The aim is to reduce effort, and increase the accuracy of collection. Regular reviews of measurement data should be arranged to make sure the data is fully exploited.

Data collection forms

The use of forms can help ensure the completeness of the primitive metrics collected and aid in the validation of the data.

Data collection forms must be simple, complete and easy to interpret. When designing forms you must consider:

- Ease of data collection – which metrics should be collected on the same form.

- Metric calculation – the number of forms from which data is needed to calculate a particular metric.

- Data analysis – the number of forms that logically go together when analysing the data.

- Validation – how easy is it to check if the data is complete and accurate.

- Administration data – project, date, configuration management data, data collector, etc. needed to verify the collected data and for long-term storage.

- Space for notes.

Support tools

Software measurement and data collection tools help to save effort in any data collection scheme. There are several commercially available tools for software measurement. As yet these do not give good support for goal-oriented measurement. You need a series of simple tools, which can often be developed in-house or built up around a spreadsheet.

Table 5.1 Example list of tools and related metrics.

Tool	Metric
Static analysis	Size, structure of code and documents, complexity
Dynamic analysis	Test coverage
Configuration management	Number of faults, run times, change requests
Project management	Schedule, costs

Such tools can provide a much more rapid response and allow metric reports to be produced more rapidly. They will also provide a greater flexibility in report format and new formats or one-off reports can be produced very rapidly.

Data collection automation can be assisted by tools that support the software development process. For example, static and dynamic analysis tools are testing tools that can also be used to produce metrics. If they are part of your existing development process they can be used to provide metrics at very little additional cost. Table 5.1 gives a list of tools and the metrics that you can collect by using them.

A measurement environment might be represented by the schematic diagram shown in Figure 5.1.

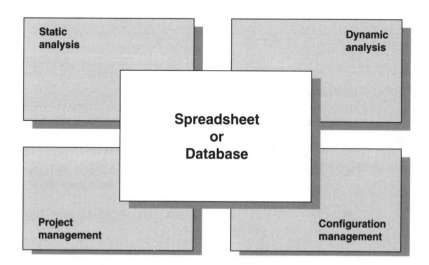

Figure 5.1 Diagram of how software tools can be used in a measurement environment.

Example: Step 8 for the Guinea Pig Project

We will use one of the forms from the Guinea Pig Project to illustrate some points of form design. The example form (Figure 5.2) is for collecting the error report log for a process. From the description of this given in the previous step you can see that this form needed to be filled in by the Development Team Leaders. The count was passed to the Quality Manager once a month. It was agreed by the Quality Manager that it would be easier if the log itself was supplied from which the Quality Manager could count the entries. To ensure that entries were not counted twice a line was drawn across the form to indicate where one month ends and another begins. The form also includes entries in date order which allowed the last error report to be identified.

M25 Page **3**	PROCESS ERROR COUNT LOG		
Process: Design and Code			
Error No.	*Date reported*	*Release*	*Comment*
25	10/02/91	DP5	Uninitialized variable
Feb 91			
28	02/03/91	DP6	Overwritten variable
36	13/03/91	DP5	Illegal input not checked

Figure 5.2 Guinea Pig Project error report log form.

Recommendations

Here are some guidelines for implementing measurement:

- Carry out regular project metrics reviews.

- Plan data collection carefully; do not underestimate the effort for collecting data items.

- Develop your new tools on widespread, commercially available products.

- Use standard interfaces for data transfer between tools.

- Use spreadsheet packages to provide one-off, easy-to-use tools.

- Prototype tools on spreadsheets.

- Use database packages with a programmable environment for large metrics programmes.

Step 9: Verifying the data

It is vital to verify the data as it becomes available. This is the time when it is easiest to correct errors and omissions. Leaving it too late can mean that you may never be able to correct it. Verification should include the following checks:

- Check the completed data collection forms for accuracy and completeness. If data is entered into a spreadsheet or database, simple data format checks, and checks to stop empty fields, can be automated.

- Look for repeated patterns that might indicate carelessness or ill-considered completion of forms. Simple graphs that a spreadsheet or database package can produce are usually sufficient for this purpose.

- Note any data values that are obviously unusual and seek explanation.

Spreadsheets and databases can provide good support for verification activities. Graphs are very effective for identifying repeated patterns and anomalous values as well as for conveying the results clearly and quickly to data collectors and project managers.

Example: Step 9 for the Guinea Pig Project

We will take the example of the process error count to illustrate what checks were performed on the Guinea Pig Project. We will take the point of view of the Quality Manager putting together the error count distribution metric. This was compiled every month. Since the Quality Manager had a list of the incoming error reports he would know how many there should be and hence an indication of the completeness of the team leaders' reports. Because the forms have slots for all the data required it is relatively easy to identify if any data is missing. By plotting the counts month by month the manager would be able to see if there were any large fluctuations that might indicate a mis-entry.

Recommendations

- Having well-designed forms and using software tools can speed up and simplify validating the data. Spreadsheets can be particularly flexible in generating graphs quickly and easily.

- If you collect the data on a regular basis you should also plan to validate it as part of the collection process.

- Careful and systematic filing of the data will help collating and retrieving it later.

Exploiting your Measures

In this chapter we see how improvement can be achieved through the exploitation of the measurement data.

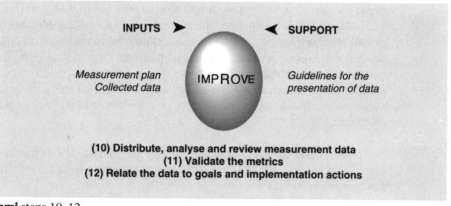

INPUTS ► ◄ SUPPORT

Measurement plan
Collected data

IMPROVE

Guidelines for the
presentation of data

(10) Distribute, analyse and review measurement data
(11) Validate the metrics
(12) Relate the data to goals and implementation actions

ami steps 10–12

Chapter 6

Fast track

Plan of action

The analysis starts with an effective presentation of the measurement data. The data is shared with those involved in the relevant goals.

Graphics must clearly show all measurement data so that both trends and outliers can be seen. Even simple statistical techniques such as averages should be used with care. The first aim in goal-oriented measurement must be to give the participants the measurement data that corresponds to their particular goals. A statistical technique or model is only to be used if appropriate – and with care.

Measurement data is then analysed. Analysis of data with goal-oriented measurement is self-referencing and fairly simple. For example, estimates use past data, error rates should tend to zero, progress should tend to 100%, and so on. However, the analysis must always be done with careful reference to the context. There is no model that can be used to say 'since the error rate has not fallen, it means that...'. Analysing in context means obtaining the background information, involving project staff and comparing the measurement data with the goals and assumptions. This analysis will validate your metrics, and you will avoid using data blindly.

By relating data to goals you will be able to identify the improvement actions and decisions that you need to take to achieve the goals that you set up.

The analysis of data will immediately help in guiding your actions. However, the metrics will also prompt you to ask more questions and then to add new goals. Goal-oriented measurement is naturally iterative since the basic motivation to improve results and increase your understanding will always be there.

Finally, although the main aim of analysis is to implement actions that control and improve the development process, it is also important to reassess the measurement plan. You can reassess the plan against the following points:

- Integration of measurement activities with other procedures

- Greater use of statistics and models

- Use of a data model and a database management system

- Corporate-wide exchange of information on goals and results

- The costs and benefits of measurement

Example: Analysing the data

To show you how the results can be analysed we will continue the example goals from the Fast track section of Chapter 4 and use goal G2: *Improve estimates*. There we identified that we wanted to collect data on the estimates and actuals for a range of projects. The scatter plot in Figure 6.1 shows the actual project effort against the estimates. The line across the graph represents where the actuals are the same as the estimates. Points lying above the line are projects that exceeded their budgets and below are those that came in under estimate.

Figure 6.1 indicates that the estimates for small projects tend to come in under the estimates while the larger ones are consistently over. However, before you start factoring all your estimates you need to check what is causing the problem. For example, it might be the case that your estimates are fine but the scope of the work changed without a corresponding change in the estimates. It would be better to ensure that estimates were updated following a change in scope. It is also sensible to examine the estimates for small projects as well for the large projects.

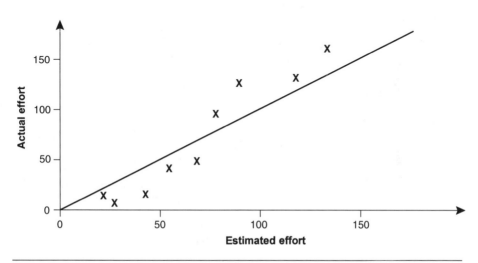

Figure 6.1 Example scatter plot of actual effort against estimated effort.

Having established your performance in estimating, you can start to look at another loop of the method to gain more information and establish better controls and understanding of the estimation process. For example, while taking the above results to indicate a need to include more contingency in your estimates, you should consider why your estimates are wrong. One thing that you might look at is whether any particular phase is being wrongly estimated.

Figure 6.2 shows a real-life example of the application of metrics. The graph illustrates Hitachi's use of measurement (Matsubara, 1991). Hitachi studied project milestones. During the final stage of projects they defined two milestones: completion of test by the QA group and the installation at the customer site.

The graph shows schedule achievement results for these milestones during a four-and-a-half year period. Almost all projects met their installation dates. For completion of the test by QA, figures are a little lower, but all scores are at least 97% for between 300 and 400 installed projects. These results are used by Hitachi to justify their investment in quality improvement and measurement over a period of several years.

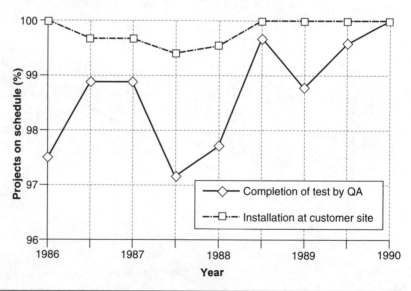

Figure 6.2 Example application of metrics by Hitachi.

Step 10: Presenting and distributing the data

 It is at this stage that the data collected is brought together for the first time and all those involved in your measurement programme can begin to see the insights it gives them into their development processes. There are two important aspects that you must consider in this step. They are the coordination of the aggregation of the results and the presentation of the results. We consider each of these in turn below.

Coordination

You will remember that in Steps 4 to 6, metrics were identified for each node of the goal tree to help answer the related questions. The metric at a particular node of a goal tree uses metrics from the lower nodes in their calculation. Also at each node you will have identified participants who have the relevant understanding of the related areas of your development process. Thus in coordinating the aggregation of your results you will need to consider the various sources and recipients of the metrics.

We would recommend that you present the results in regular measurement reports that summarize the metrics collected and comments on the interpretation of the results from the participants. The advantages of producing a report are:

- It provides a permanent record of the results.

- It provides a suitable way of distributing the results.

- It ensures that all the participants are fully informed and encourages them to remain committed to the programme.

The frequency at which you will be able to produce the report will depend on

- the extent of data collection – the more sources of data you use the longer it will take to bring it all together;

- the number of levels in your goal tree.

As metrics are aggregated and you progress up the tree, you might choose to present them to the participants involved in the goal tree at the level you are currently processing. They will be able to comment on any anomalies in the values. The comments can be incorporated into your metrics report as supporting comments to the results. They will provide further valuable insights and will help the initiator in analysing the results.

Statistical analysis versus graphs

The choice of how to present and exploit the data needs to be made with the assistance of the metrics promoter or someone with experience of this type of activity. Data representation and analysis should be kept simple. Avoid complicated statistical techniques and models for the following reasons:

- Many software models are immature and difficult to apply. The possible exceptions to this are **cost models** and **reliability models** which are becoming more widely accepted and are discussed at the end of this chapter.

- You will need to calibrate statistical models. This typically requires a large volume of historical data and a detailed knowledge of the relevant development processes used. Very few organizations are likely to have enough data to do this.

- If an experiment is set up within a software project, you will need to design it very carefully using staff who are experienced in the design of experiments. Software projects rarely fit the standard experimental criteria of yielding normally distributed data. Further, it can be very difficult to set up a number of projects which are sufficiently similar to allow proper comparisons to be made.

- Even when a statistical test is applied, there is always a degree of uncertainty associated with the result. You will require experience and understanding of the project and company context to interpret the results.

For these reasons we would recommend graphical analysis which will give you the following advantages:

- It is robust because there are no underlying statistical assumptions.

- It is user-friendly because graphs convey information more clearly and do not deter people in the same way as statistical terms.

Nevertheless, the selection of the information to be plotted must still be made with care and the interpretation of the graphs carried out carefully. The plots used to analyse the results need to be carefully tailored to provide the best support for specific goals. Tools should be used to save time and ensure accuracy. In considering what type of plot to use it is important to understand that each type of data or metric used to support a particular goal has a presentation that eases the task of assimilation of the data. You may also need to take into account that a manager may prefer certain types of data plotted in a particular way. In this case it may be better to follow the existing practice of your organization.

Types of graphical presentation

An important decision in putting the metrics report together is how to present the results. There is a wide range of ways of presenting data graphically and this can make it difficult to decide which one to use. Below we show you some formats that have been found by experience to be the most useful and explain their advantages.

The types of plots most widely used in practice are: histograms, pie charts, scatter plots and X-t plots. You may find that sometimes the use of more than one type of plot can prove useful. There follow examples of the various formats of plots and indications of the situations where these are likely to be of advantage.

Pie chart

This sort of diagram will highlight very large or very small percentage items and gives a visual indication of the balance between the proportions of the constituent parts.

Figure 6.3 is an example of the use of a pie chart to show the percentage of problem reports per function tested where A to G represent the functions tested. It clearly shows that D generated nearly half the problem reports and indicates a potential problem associated with this function. However, this is not conclusive evidence that function D is really a problem. The example histogram in Figure 6.4 also shows how, by changing the presentation and comparing additional measures, further insights can be gained.

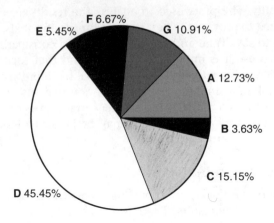

Figure 6.3 Example of a pie chart, showing percentage of problem notes per function tested.

Histogram

This sort of diagram will show the relative values of a number of quantities and, as in the example, between pairs or groups of values.

Figure 6.4 gives an example of the use of a histogram used to show the number of test scenarios versus the number of problem reports.

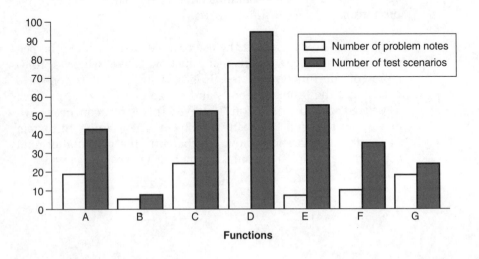

Figure 6.4 Example of a histogram.

With the example pie chart given in Figure 6.3 we concluded that either function D is susceptible to errors or the test scenarios have not exercised the functionality sufficiently. The histogram helps us to see that D has had a lot of testing. On the other hand, the test scenarios used seem to have had little impact on E, though this might be because of the inability of these scenarios to test it.

X-t plots

This sort of diagram will show how a number of quantities vary with time and helps identify any trends that are linked to time.

Figure 6.5 shows an X-t plot of the actual and estimated effort for a project that has just completed its coding phase. The trend of actuals against estimates shows a consistent under-estimate. The indication is that the next phases will also go over the estimate. This needs urgent investigation since the next phases are proportionally larger.

Scatter plots

Scatter plots allow you to see if there are trends between two measures and how well values are grouped. Figure 6.6 is an example of a scatter plot used to show the effort expended against delivered lines of code. What you are likely to be looking for is some sort of correlation between these measures to help in estimating future projects. As shown by Figure 6.6, the values do not lie exactly on a curve and

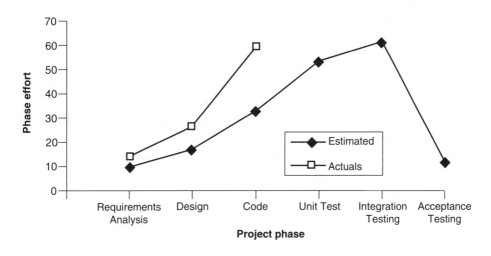

Figure 6.5 Example of an X-t plot.

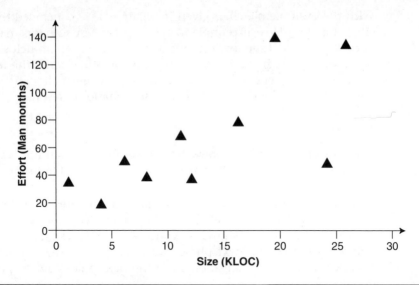

Figure 6.6 Example of a scatter plot.

any prediction has a degree of uncertainty. For a discussion of the problems associated with trying to identify trends in this sort of data see Fenton (1991) and Boehm (1981).

Based on experience, we found that certain types of plot are favoured for certain types of data. Table 6.1 summarizes the main ones.

When using graphs to identify relationships between measures take care to validate that the relationship is true and not just some accident of fate. For example, if you are looking at the relationship of actual effort against lines of code for a number of projects to establish a basis for estimating future projects, you could find that there is a good correlation between these two measures. However, this could be because the projects are of a specific type. The projects you will be estimating may be of a different type and not fit the trend identified in the projects used for correlation.

Example: Step 10 for the Guinea Pig Project

In the Guinea Pig Project the Metrics Promoter was given the responsibility for collecting the basic metrics from the Team Leaders and presenting them to the Project Manager.

Table 6.1 Types of plot suitable for different sorts of data.

Type of data	Type of plot	Data used
Resource usage e.g. effort, elapse time, computer time	X-t plot Pie chart Scatter plot	Resource usage against time Resource usage for each phase Estimates against actuals
System size	X-t plot X-t plot X-t plot	Change of estimate with time System size with time System size with phase
Document size	X-t plot X-t plot X-t plot	Change of estimate with time Document size with time Document size with phase
Source code size	X-t plot X-t plot	Code size against time % code/phase against time
Code complexity	Scatter plot Histogram	Code size against complexity Complexity against module
Test coverage	Scatter plot X-t plot	Test coverage against no. of faults discovered per unit time Test coverage against time
No. of faults	X-t plot Histogram Histogram	Error rate against time No. of faults against sub-system No. of faults against module
Number of changes	X-t plot Scatter plot	Cumulative no. of changes per line of code against time No. of changes against no. of faults
Requirements changes	X-t plot	No. of changes per phase
Structure metrics e.g. no. of calls; no. of I/O variables; no. of decisions per unit	Pie chart or Histogram	Structure metric versus module Average structure metric per module for each sub-system
Qualitative data e.g. quality of documentation	Pie chart or Histogram	Value versus unit (e.g. document, module)

In deciding how to present the metrics, the Metrics Promoter had to bear in mind the aspects that would be of interest to the Project Manager as well as the need to support the goals and questions set in the measurement programme. In the Guinea Pig Project, sub-goals SG2 and SG3 indicate the interest is in quality as indicated in the errors and how the processes contribute to the quality. Thus one way used to present the information was to plot the relative values of the error counts for each process.

We will take as an example the data on the errors detected per process for a given release shown in Table 6.2 as received from the Team Leaders. One way used to present this data was as a pie chart since they were interested in the relative proportions of the error detection of the various phases. A sample presentation is shown in Figure 6.7. This would have been distributed to the Project Manager with copies sent to the Team Leaders and Quality Manager.

Table 6.2 Guinea Pig Project error detection counts.

M12: ERROR DETECTION COUNTS

Release DP5.   Date: 30/11/91

Process	Count	Percentage
Requirements analysis	10	6.0
Design and code	23	13.8
Module test	58	35.0
Integration test	73	44.0
Acceptance test	2	1.2
TOTAL	166	100.0

An alternative presentation is to use a histogram and an example of this is shown in the example for Step 12 (see Figure 6.8) where it is used as part of the interpretation of the data.

Recommendations

Here are some recommendations that will help you decide how to present your results:

- When plotting against time, indications of the life-cycle phases and of the major events of the project are important.

- Pie charts are often used to report percentage figures, for example the percentage of test coverage for each function or the percentage of errors due to each phase of the life cycle.

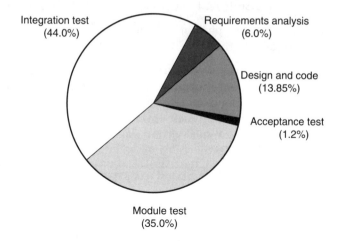

Figure 6.7 Pie chart for error detection rates from Table 6.2.

- If a series of plots are being used for analysing a set of data, take care to use a consistent set of scales, colours, etc.

- Histograms are used when comparison is needed, for example forecast against actuals; problems observed against number of test scenarios run; and number of failures observed against number of changes.

- Outliers must be treated with care. You should justify why they should be considered as atypical, and why they can be omitted from further analysis.

- Try to present simple plots; proving relationships between several metrics is generally difficult.

- When investigating the relationship between two variables, inspect the scatter plot visually; furthermore, use robust correlation coefficients to confirm whether a relationship exists.

Step 11: Validating the metrics

Validating the metrics means showing that they are adequate for the purpose required of them. The metrics presented must allow you to make deductions about your development processes and enable you to identify ways in which they can be improved. In validating the metrics the sorts of things that you need to check include:

- There is sufficient data to allow trends to be identified.

- The data is typical of your processes. If there are any abnormal conditions these need to be identified.

- The presence of confounding factors that will need to be taken into account in analysing your data: for example, if you are collecting cumulative error rates and testing has not been completed. In this case it would be dangerous to make full use of this data to make deductions about the total number of errors in the project.

- Do the values correspond to the participants' intuitive feel for their expected magnitude? Where there is a difference you will need to investigate to ensure the values reflect the real situation.

The results of these investigations need to be included in the metrics reports supplied to the initiator and the participants when they are analysing the metrics.

Outliers should be identified and a decision made on how to treat them. Outliers are values that lie outside the range of the mass of other data that you have collected. They should not simply be ignored. They give valuable hints to problems with assumptions made about your data. They should be carefully investigated and what makes them different identified: for example, if you are looking at the relationship of effort and lines of delivered code for a number of projects. An outlier might indicate, for example, a project that uses a different life cycle. Once you have identified the difference you will know that this type of project does not fit with the others. In predicting effort for such projects you will need to examine them more carefully than the others.

Validating the metrics can be either objective or subjective. For the objective validation a trend can usually be derived through experience or via experience reports from outside the company. In subjective validation those involved in the process are asked for their subjective opinions as to whether the data matches their intuitive feel of what actually took place.

Example: Step 11 for the Guinea Pig Project

We will take the example of the metric used in Step 10. This is intended to help with the sub-goal 3: *to understand better the level of quality of the products produced by the various processes*. The project used the intuitive idea that the fewer the errors detected down-stream the better the processes upstream are likely to be. There are a number of things that could go wrong with this assumption. It could have been invalidated if one phase of the life cycle is not complete before the next starts. For example, integration testing starts before module testing is complete and both the module test team and integration team are testing the same piece of software. Again, if the customer is not really using the delivered software then this might give an artificially low level of customer error reports.

Another problem might be caused by faulty configuration management, in which case errors already cleared have not been properly propagated to the next process and the same error is detected twice.

It was the responsibility of the metrics promoter to talk to the team leaders to verify that none of these sorts of things occurred.

Recommendations

- Be on the lookout for unusual and unexpected values and follow them up immediately. If you delay too long the evidence may have disappeared.

- Try to relate the trends to your understanding of events in the project. If you can think of no explanation, it could be an indication of problems of which the project is unaware.

- Make use of other people's experience to help interpret the results.

Step 12: Relating data to goals

This is the last step of the **ami** method and here we shall analyse what the data indicates and produce action plans for what you want to do next. This section is focused on the activities for the first time through the **ami** method loop. These will be simpler than for later loops. A later section entitled 'Strategies for Improvement' describes in more detail how you can use the analysis once you have some experience of applying the **ami** method and would like to be more ambitious.

The main input to the analysis of the results is the measurement report. You will be looking at the metrics to give you an insight into your development processes and using the goals to focus your analysis. The sorts of things that the results will be used for are

- normal values associated with the processes such as the level of productivity. This would normally be associated with knowledge goals;

- trends that will help you predict future projects. This would normally be associated with knowledge goals;

- trends that indicate that a project might get into trouble, for example higher than expected error rates during testing on a set of modules might indicate that they may need special attention. This would normally be associated with control goals.

The range of things that you will be looking for will be mainly determined by your goals.

We need to sound a note of caution here. The metrics will provide only an *indication*. There may be good reasons for the distribution of errors without the process being wrong. Before action is taken to change any process, you should look at the circumstances and decide if there really is something amiss. It is important to understand that the metrics are indicators of potential problems. They must only be used as part of the evidence and not proof that a problem exists.

It is important that you use the data to make decisions to improve your processes. If you do not make that commitment at the start of the initiative then you will be in danger of not taking the initiative seriously and wasting money because not enough thought was given to selecting the most pertinent data. It is also the reason for identifying those responsible for the entities when you put your goal tree together. They will be able to make changes in the processes for which they have responsibility.

We have already pointed out that one difficulty for software data comes from the poor validity for the classical assumptions of data distribution (i.e. Gaussian). Nevertheless, relationships among metrics can be determined through robust or multivariate regression. The objective of it is to identify whether a relationship exists between the dependent variable and explanatory variables and, if so, to predict the dependent variable from the explanatory variables for new data.

It has been observed that software data is heavily skewed, has an increasing variance and a relatively high number of outliers. As a consequence, robust summary statistics provide a more accurate representation of the data.

Including subjective data

During Step 12, subjective data can be considered with objective results. These are based on an individual's or a group's feeling or understanding of a certain characteristic or condition or event. They can also serve as corroboration of the objective data. Subjective data provide critical additional information for interpreting the initiative results and support for investigations.

A good example of this is the analysis of continuous schedule slippage of a project. The development effort data collected to monitor productivity might show several re-estimations of the remaining effort to finish the project and each time the previous estimation is identified as insufficient. A worthwhile subjective metric could be the volume of requirements changes requested by the customer throughout the project life (that is, after requirements specifications have been accepted) which were not correctly formalized and, consequently, not well recorded.

Finally, relating data to goals can frequently be used to predict. The use of metrics for prediction rests on the assumption that the metric measures an inherent property of the software and a relationship exists between the inherent property and the final product's performance.

Step 12 of the **ami** method should lead to corrections of the assessment conducted within Step 1. If not, the measurement plan in this first loop of the **ami** approach was not really efficient. The goals or sub-goals might not have been properly matched to the context and learning from the results is typically not satisfactory.

Example: Step 12 for the Guinea Pig Project

We will again use the example from Step 10. Figure 6.8 gives an example of a display of a different set of error data as a histogram used on the Guinea Pig Project. It includes two sets of data to allow comparison; one is an analysis of customer error reports and the other of errors detected in the different processes.

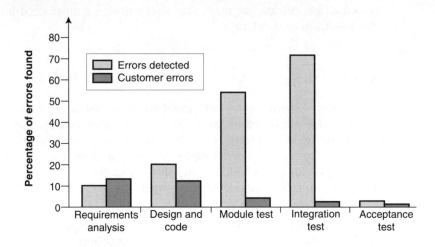

Figure 6.8 Example of a histogram from the Guinea Pig Project.

We will now look at how these metrics were interpreted. The pie chart given in Step 10 (Figure 6.7) was used to support SG2: *to understand better where errors are introduced.* The distribution of values is roughly what they would expect if things were working as expected. There is a small number of errors detected in requirements analysis and design, a large volume in module test and integration test and then small amounts in acceptance testing and from customer reports.

There would be several situations that would have caused concern for the Project Manager. This would include things like high levels in acceptance testing and customer reports. High levels in acceptance testing would imply that the product was being put into acceptance testing too early or that the integration tests were not thorough enough. This would clearly point to a need to investigate the cause. If there were high levels of customer reports then the customer is unlikely to be happy with the product. This might indicate that integration testing or acceptance testing was not adequate.

The histogram was used to support SG3: *to understand better the level of quality of the products produced by the different processes.* The customer error data shows that the requirements specification gave rise to the same number of problems as the design and code. It might be expected that in most projects the requirement errors should be less than the design and code errors. There may be a potential problem with the requirements analysis process. When we look at the error detection rate of requirements analysis this is low. One could infer from this that the requirements analysis process is not producing the right quality of product.

Recommendations

The following recommendations will help you with the assessment of your results:

- Do not be over-ambitious for your first set of results. Perfection is never achieved the first time.

- Make use of the knowledge gained from the trends shown by the metrics. Identify the specific actions to put your project or company on an improved course.

- Consider verifying your observations via an external audit. An expert may identify complementary key items that are impeding the efficiency of your development process.

- Report the results obtained to all participants of the measurement initiative. They have put much effort into collecting the data and will be interested in the fruits of their labour. If you do not provide results to them they may become demotivated and be difficult to remotivate.

- Obtain the reactions to the results from the people directly connected with the development process. They are likely to provide further insights and provide more pragmatic proposals for improvement.

- To continue the momentum of the measurement initiative, it is important that the way forward, and why this is important for the company, is carefully explained.

- Report on the cost of the measurement initiative. The people involved in the initiative will be interested in this and you might well be able to surprise them with the small relative cost of the measurement programme.

- Identify the difficulties encountered and ask for suggestions for improvement.

- Don't stop the initiative without justification; such an action can be misinterpreted.

Strategies for improvement

We have now completed the last step in the **ami** method. In Chapter 4, we derived metrics to answer the questions in the goal tree. In Chapter 5 the goals and questions were recorded in a plan for the implementation of a measurement programme. Having validated the metrics against any assumptions or models used, we can use them to assess the goals of the measurement plan and produce an action plan for improvement.

Software measurement is an iterative process – the more you collect, the better you know how to collect and what to collect. Two objectives are part of the strategy of improvement:

● To quantify the benefits from any measurement programme.

● To improve the return on investment made.

One simple way to do this is to set up a permanent database and feed in data from every project involved in data collection. In this way, data is treated as a resource for the whole organization, and more sophisticated data analysis and reporting facilities can be considered.

By Step 12 of the **ami** method you will have added to your understanding of your development process and provided yourself with ideas on how to improve them. Where you started will determine what your next step is likely to be. If you have basic knowledge goals you might consider putting in more detailed metrics to start to identify process improvements. If you have improvement goals then having identified your improvements you will want to measure your gain in efficiency and add to your existing set of metrics and goals to identify further improvements.

If you did your assessment using the SEI questionnaire, you might like to revisit the assessment to check if your processes have improved. If you started at a low maturity level it may take a few iterations of the method before you see an improvement in your maturity level. If you are already improving your process it may give you an indication of additional areas.

If you started your measurement initiative with only a few projects you might consider including more in the next loop. The cost of extending to more projects will certainly be less than your first application of the method because you will be able to reuse much of the original material.

Later, when you have accumulated more historic data, you might consider using further analysis using models. A model postulates a relation between two or more measures. The two most used models are cost models and reliability models.

Cost models are usually based on data collected from a large number of different projects. The general assumption is that cost is in some way related to size; the difficulty comes from the evaluation of the size of a system that does not yet exist. Several techniques have been tested, none being entirely satisfactory. Cost drivers (that is, coefficients for adaptation) represent attributes of the development environment, type of project and resources profiles.

Reliability models are usually based on an analysis of failures in terms of the mean time between failures. General assumptions are made with these models about the independence of failures and the way that errors are fixed. This assumption is an approximation. The way that this affects the results of the analysis using this model needs to be considered when interpreting the results.

The use of a statistical model supposes a high level of maturity (that is, level 3 of the SEI assessment in which the software process is completely understood and monitored) and this is the reason it was not introduced in Chapter 4. The use of a statistical model will improve the results only if calibration is possible with existing data.

Software models will not be discussed further here. There is much specialized literature available. A brief guide to some of the more important references in this area is given in Chapter 7.

Example: Strategies for improvement for the Guinea Pig Project

These are early days in collecting metrics for the Guinea Pig Project. Having established some baselines they can now compare deliveries and gain an idea of when things have gone wrong and, more important, when things are going wrong. It was important for the Guinea Pig Project to go through a number of deliveries to establish a trend in the metric values before trying to improve.

How should the Guinea Pig Project use the metric data to help direct its improvement strategies? First, the metrics will help identify areas that can be tidied up. For example, in the histogram analysis in Step 12 they identified requirement analysis as a potential problem area. The project manager can carry out a review of the procedures used in requirements analysis and identify where it could be improved. It might be that its configuration management procedures need to be tightened up or that there is a need for more reviews. This must be established by investigation. When the procedures are changed, the project should continue to collect the metrics to establish that the changes have improved the product quality.

As the understanding of those involved in the project improves, they can start thinking of adding to the goals. For example, now they have a feeling of the level of customer error reports, they can begin considering setting a target of reducing this.

It is too early for the Guinea Pig Project to consider using models. At this stage the project should be concentrating on raising its maturity level. The application of the SEI questionnaire will have indicated the areas where the project needs to improve to raise its maturity. The Project Manager is best advised to construct a 'shopping list' of things that need to be improved to raise the maturity level of the project. These should be gradually introduced into the project while continuing to measure the same metrics and possibly adding more.

The prognosis for the Guinea Pig Project is good. Those involved are now beginning to get a feel for the levels of errors arising in the various processes and the levels of errors detected. Over several deliveries they will have established the trends and will have got a feel for when things are going wrong. They can introduce improvements into areas that have been highlighted by the metrics and are able to measure the effect of the improvements. They are building a firm foundation upon which further improvements can be introduced in a controlled manner.

Further Reading

Chapter 7

Other approaches

With the **ami** approach, goals are used to derive the metrics needed by an organization. Two alternative approaches are also in use. It is necessary to have some idea of these other approaches, because you will probably come across them, and in any case, they are, to some extent, complementary.

The first is often called the bottom-up data collection approach. Data from an experimental or pilot project is collected and then analysed to find correlations or interesting trends. This is used to derive the metrics, but it can be time-consuming and wasteful. It is a very expensive procedure with costs as high as 30% of development costs, so it is not a recommended approach. Furthermore it can often lead to failure as it does not reflect specific goals.

The second approach is to use a predefined model, which defines the metrics and how the measurement data is to be interpreted. In some cases the model is flexible and allows a certain choice of metrics. Some disadvantages are encountered when using predefined models. These models aim to be general purpose, and the number of metrics that have to be collected is fairly high. An example is Kitchenham's Constructive Quality Model (Kitchenham, 1987) which defines quality factors of the software product and derives the metrics. The metrics are used to control or evaluate the quality of the software product. The cost of application is reported to be around 10% of development costs. Data collectors can suffer from lack of motivation as they realize that not all the metrics are useful. Even though they define a large number of metrics, the characteristics of the model often exclude the collection of other very useful data.

Such models are often difficult to use. An example is the COCOMO model for estimating project productivity (Boehm, 1981), which uses a large number of parameters to make estimates. The user of the model sets the level of the parameters and the model estimates productivity using past project data. However, the parameters are difficult to set and the resulting metrics are not easy to interpret correctly.

These predefined models are used in a number of different situations. An example is in safety-critical systems where the most important quality requirement is very clear. Customers will often push for the use of a model such as Kitchenham's Constructive Quality Model (or equivalent ones – see Forse (1989)) even if they are costly and difficult to exploit efficiently.

Goal-oriented measurement is a very general framework. Controlled use of experimental data collection or of particular models can be beneficially exploited within this framework. Using these approaches within a goal-oriented framework can reduce the problems associated with them.

Goal-oriented measurement is not without disadvantages. Developing a measurement plan and exploiting the data requires commitment from all those involved, especially the managers who initiate measurement and participants who use the data. While goal-oriented measurement may not appear to be the easiest approach to use initially, its practicality and transparency of purpose does achieve success.

Further reading

The **ami** handbook is a self-contained description of a method for using quantitative approaches in software development. As you start applying the method you may want to find out more about specific subjects in the area of software measurement. Measurement is a technique that supports other activities and so is also related to other areas of software development (Figure 7.1).

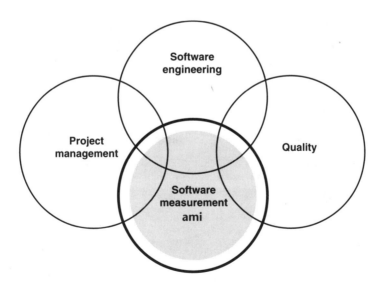

Figure 7.1 Support for measurement from other areas.

The following sections give some useful references related to all four areas.

Software measurement

When using **ami** you may want more information on specific metrics and models. You will also find that case studies are useful for motivating people and giving guidance. Several different ESPRIT projects have developed complementary material to promote and support the use of metrics. The relationship between the main projects is shown in Figure 7.2.

The METKIT project produces educational and training packages on software measurement. The documentation for these modules is *Software Metrics* (Fenton, 1991). The book is complementary to the **ami** handbook. **ami** emphasizes a systematic approach through an organization's use of a method and a measurement plan. METKIT emphasizes rigour in metrics definition and in measurement data interpretation. A good alternative to Fenton is the *Software Reliability Handbook* edited by P. Rook (1990) which, despite its title, covers most aspects of measurement. It is a collection of articles by the same authors who collaborated on the Fenton book.

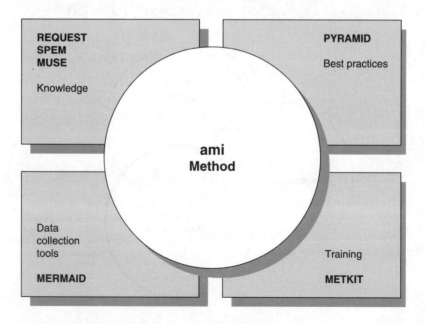

Figure 7.2 ESPRIT support for your measurement programme.

The **ami** project has produced training material for the **ami** method covering the content of the handbook. The training is aimed at giving an overview of the **ami** method and how it relates to measurement. A more advanced course is also available which will teach metrics promoters and similar people how to apply the **ami** method.

The best practice guide (Moeuller, 1992), the Hewlett-Packard experience (Grady, 1987; Cox, 1991), the TAME project (Basili, 1988), and the Japanese experience (Matsubara, 1991) are all useful for understanding present and future trends in software measurement.

If you are intending to measure the effectiveness of new methods or tools in your projects, the DESMET project (Law, 1992) has produced material and advice on how to do it. The DESMET approach employs the **ami** method.

From projects to processes

Brooks's *The Mythical Man-Month* (1975) is still a classic text on the problems of managing software. A project can be broken down into logically related tasks, each of which is allocated a specific number of man-months. This is a standard technique that works well in construction or manufacturing where each task is supported by a design document. The definition of a design task and a testing task is very much less clear. Hence the mythical nature of many project plans and the corresponding budgeted (and measured) man-months.

More modern attempts treat tasks as processes. An example of this approach is *Managing the Software Process* (Humphreys, 1989). However, the debate continues on how best to match creative design work to project plans and processes.

Risk management (Boehm, 1991) is important and is a complementary technique to SEI process improvement, especially for organizations at a low maturity level with high risks.

Kitchenham gives perceptive reviews of some cost estimating models in Rook (1990).

Approaches to quality

Several different but largely complementary approaches to quality are now extensively used.

Juran (1988) stresses the management of quality at all phases in the product life cycle. This builds the link at the management level between quality and productive activities. This approach gives a good environment in which to undertake measurement.

Crosby (1979) stresses the importance of involvement and motivation for everyone within an organization. He proposed a five-level maturity grid for the improvement of quality that is a precursor to SEI's software capability maturity levels. He also shows how the cost of quality and of non-conformance can be measured.

Deming (1982) stresses the technical and scientific aspects of quality, especially statistics and experiment plans. He gives advice on how to measure work processes.

ISO 9000 is becoming the European standard for quality system certification. Measurement is a useful complement since metrics can give the information on quality improvement and performance that is lacking within ISO 9000. DOD2176A (1988) is another widely used standard in software development.

Software engineering

The software engineering techniques used vary from country to country and from one application area to another. There is no standard European text in this area, but there are plenty of texts in different languages.

Issues of software engineering are found in Humphreys (1989) and in the *Software Reliability Handbook* (Rook, 1990). The SEI reports should be read by those wishing to make extensive use of the SEI model, especially SEI (1991).

Experience of using the **ami** method

Following the completion of the **ami** project, the companies in the **ami** consortium continued to use the **ami** method. Some of their experiences have been written up in published papers and cover experiences from a number of industries and companies:

- Debou (1992) describes the experience of Alcatel in a large telecommunications project;

- Liptak (1992) describes the experience of Alcatel in the space industry;

- the experiences of GEC on a number of radar and real-time projects is summarized in Pulford (1995);

- Debou (1994) describes two applications of the **ami** method in the telecommunications and railway signalling areas, and with using **ami** to aid achieving ISO 9000 certification.

A number of companies outside the **ami** consortium have now adopted the **ami** method. The experiences described in Debou (1994) involve the use of the **ami** method supported by Objectif Technology. Bacon (1994) describes the adoption of **ami** by an assurance company.

Recommended books and papers

Bacon, S. (1994). **ami** at PROVINCIAL MUTUAL LAA. *De Facto,* **(7)**, January

> This article describes how Provincial Mutual, a medium-sized life and pensions office, adopted the **ami** method to implement its measurement programme.

Basili, V. R. and Rombach, D. (1988). The TAME project: towards improvement-orientated software environments. *IEEE Trans. Soft. Eng.,* **14**(6), 758–73

> Describes the Basili G/Q/M approach. Also presents research into integrated support environments for goal-oriented measurement.

Boehm, B.W. (1981). *Software Engineering Economics.* Prentice-Hall

> A well-known text that presents the COCOMO cost models and the TRW projects measurement database from which they were derived.

Boehm, B.W. and Royce, W. (1989). COCOMO Ada et le modèle de dévelopement Ada. *Génie Logiciel et Systèmes Experts,* **17**, 36–53

> The results of the calibration of the COCOMO model for Ada projects. The projects have a very narrow range of productivities that does not justify the large number of parameters in the model. But the cost model can be useful for evaluating

the factors that contribute to cost as well as for making predictions.

Boehm, B.W. (1991). Software risk management: principles and practices. *IEEE Software*, January, 32–41

Projects that do not have a well-defined process have high risks. Effective control on such projects comes from good risk management. This article summarizes Boehm's work on the subject.

Brooks, F.P. (1975). *The Mythical Man-Month*. Addison-Wesley

An early text on the problems of controlling large software projects.

International Business Week (1991). The quality imperative. McGraw-Hill, 2 December, 18–83

A series of articles reviewing world-wide current practices in quality. Includes some articles on software quality.

Card, D. and Glass, R. (1990). *Measuring Software Design Quality*. Prentice-Hall

Describes design-oriented measurement.

Cox, G. (1991). Sustaining a metrics programme in industry. In *Software Reliability and Metrics* (Littlewood, B. and Fenton, N., eds). Elsevier

Based on recent Hewlett-Packard corporate experience in software measurement. It shows how different participants within the development process need to use different metrics.

Crosby, P.B. (1979). *Quality is free*. McGraw-Hill

A very readable, American best-seller on how to motivate for achieving quality. Crosby's approach makes extensive use of a maturity grid and of the measurement of non-conformances and of the cost of quality.

Debou, C., Kuntzmann-Combelles, A. and Rowe, A. (1994). A Quantitative Approach to Software Management. In *Proceedings* 2nd International Software Metrics Symposium. IEEE Computer Society: London, October

This describes two applications of the **ami** method in the telecommunications and railway signalling industries. It includes descriptions of the goals and sub-goals used.

Debou, C., Pescoller, L. and Fuchs, N. (1992). Software Measurement on Telecoms Systems – Success Stories. In *Proceedings*, 3rd European Conference on Software Quality. Madrid, November

Covers the introduction of measurement on telecommunications systems using the **ami** method. It includes the strategy they used and provides some of the concrete results they obtained.

Deming, W.E. (1982). *Out of the Crisis*. MIT Press

A synthesis of Deming's approach to quality. The **ami** approach is similar to his Plan–Do–Check–Act cycle for improvement (or Shewhart cycle). **ami** has taken this cycle, based on common-sense principles, and developed it for software measurement.

DOD2167A (1988). *DOD-STD-1267A: Military Standard*. Defense System Software Development

A widely used standard for software development.

Fenton, N. (1991). *Software Metrics: a Rigorous Approach*. Chapman & Hall

A systematic presentation of software metrics and models. The classification scheme of resource, product and process metrics is used to organize the material in the book. A third of the book is written by contributing authors.

Forse, T. (1989). *Qualimétrie des Systèmes Complexes*. Les Editions d'Organisation

An example of quality measurement based on the factor/criteria/metrics model.

Gilb, T. and Graham, D. (1933). Software Inspection. Addison-Wesley

> Gives advice on how metrics from document and code inspections can be used to measure document and code quality and how these can be exploited to improve the development process.

Grady, R.B. and Caswell, D.L. (1987). *Software metrics: Establishing a Company-wide Program*. Prentice-Hall

> A very readable and interesting presentation of the Hewlett-Packard experience with software measurement.

Humphreys, W.S. (1989). *Managing the Software Process*. Addison-Wesley

> The author is the leader of the SEI initiative on the Software Capability Maturity Model. The book gives a detailed presentation of software engineering principles, the Maturity Model and the uses of measurement.

ISO9000-3. *ISO 9000-3 Guidelines for the Application of ISO9001 to the Development, Supply and Maintenance of Software.*

> Part of a series of standards for certifying an organization's quality management system.

Juran, J.M. (1988). *Juran on Planning for Quality.* Free Press Macmillan

> Gives the principles for quality management of work processes and hence for achieving the business objectives of profitability and customer satisfaction. Juran was very influential in Japan. His approach also underlies the principles of such standards as ISO 9000. The **ami** approach also takes a process-centred perspective.

Kitchenham, B. and de Neumann, B. (1990). Cost modelling and estimating. In *Software Reliability Handbook* (Rook, P., ed.). Elsevier

> Reviews an important area of software project management.

Kitchenham, B. and Pickard L. (1987). Towards a constructive quality model. Part II: statistical techniques for modelling software quality in the ESPRIT REQUEST project. *Software Eng. J.*, July, 114–26

An example of quality measurement based on the Factor/Criteria/Metrics model.

Law, D. and Naeem, T. (1992). DESMET: Determining an evaluation methodology for software methods and tools. In *CASE: Current Practice and Future Prospects* (Spurr K. and Layzel P., eds). Wiley.

This describes an approach to evaluating software methods and tools which uses the **ami** method.

Liptak, J. and Fuchs, N. (1992). Introducing and using goal-oriented software measurement programmes within a space software development environment. In *Proceedings*, Eurometrics 92. Brussels, April

This describes an approach to measurement developed by Alcatel Austria for the European Space Agency and based on the **ami** method.

Littlewood, B. and Fenton, N. (eds) (1991). *Software Reliability and Metrics*. Elsevier

A recent collection of articles.

Moeuller, K.H. and Paulish, D.J. (1992). *Software Metrics: A Practitioner's Guide to Improved Product Development*. Chapman & Hall

Gives some case studies of metrics use in Europe. The **ami** method can be used for implementing the advice in this report.

Matsubara, T. (1991). Project Management in Japan. *American Programmer*, June, 41–50

Gives some details of Hitachi's approach to software measurement and improvement. Also reviews the current state of Japanese software factories. Destroys many myths that are propagated in the US about these factories.

METKIT (1992). METKIT Software Engineering Measurement Teaching Materials. Academic modules published by South Bank University, London SE1 0AA, UK; industrial modules published by Brameur Ltd, Clark House, Kings Road, Fleet, GU13 9AD, UK.

These are a series of teaching modules developed to introduce the concepts of metrics and their application. These modules are available for licence from the above organizations. More information is available on Web page URL: http://www.sbu.ac.uk/~csse/metkit.html.

Musa, J., Iannino, A. and Okumoto, K. (1987). *Software Reliability: Measurement, Prediction and Application.* McGraw-Hill

Describes reliability-oriented measurement.

MUSE (1989). *MUSE Handbook.* ESPRIT project, unpublished

Results from the MUSE project on goal-oriented measurement and basic metrics were reused by the **ami** project.

Pulford, K. and Hollom, J. (1995). Experience of Software Measurement Programmes and Application of the **ami** Method within GEC. *The GEC Journal of Research,* **12** (1), 17–25

The experience within GEC of using metrics and the **ami** method on radar and real-time systems is described. It includes example metrics and results from the metrics' programmes.

REQUEST (1989). REQUEST *data analysis report.* ESPRIT project, unpublished

Results on data analysis were reused by the **ami** project.

Rombach, H.D. (1991). Practical benefits of goal-oriented measurement. In *Software Reliability and Metrics* (Littlewood, B. and Fenton, N., eds). Elsevier

Presents templates that are used to automate goal-oriented measurement in the TAME environment.

Rook, P. (ed.) (1990). *Software Reliability Handbook.* Elsevier

Despite the restrictive title, this book contains a wide range ofinteresting articles on software engineering and measurement.

SEI (1987). *A Method for Assessing the Software Engineering Capability of Contractors.* Technical Report CMU/SEI-87-TR-23. Software Engineering Institute, Carnegie Mellon University

Presents the assessment questions that are reproduced in Appendix 1.

SEI (1991). *Capability Maturity Model for Software.* Technical Report CMU/SEI-91-TR-24. Software Engineering Institute, Carnegie Mellon University

> A new version of the SEI maturity model. It identifies key practice areas for process improvement.

SEI Process Assessment

In September 1987 the Software Engineering Institute (SEI) released a technical report (SEI, 1987) that generated considerable public interest. The SEI report proposed a five-level capability maturity model in which each level must be stabilized before improvement to the next level can be attempted. The report provides a list of assessment questions and gives the scoring mechanism for deriving the maturity level of a project or organization. It also gives a set of guidelines for conducting the assessment process. A more recent report (SEI, 1991) gives guidelines on how to use the model for improving your engineering practice.

This appendix presents the questions and shows you how to assess your maturity level. You will also find the scoring mechanism, assessment procedure, follow-up questions, and certain key terms from the 1987 SEI technical report. Advice on customizing the assessment process is also given.

Assessment

Results have shown that the great majority of organizations and projects are at level 1, the lowest level. Two points need to be emphasized.

(1)   Assessing your maturity level, in the context of the **ami** Metrics Users Handbook, should be seen in its true light – as a step to determining the improvement goals appropriate for your organization.

(2)   You should review your results against each section of the SEI questionnaire. The sections represent areas of engineering practice. You can then see your weak areas and derive improvement goals – in effect, regarding the maturity level merely as an indicator.

The July 1991 issue of *IEEE Software* discusses software capability evaluation (SCE) issues.

SEI assessment procedure

The SEI recommends creating an assessment team and using the following procedure. This recommended procedure assumes a software organization has a number of projects in various stages of development.

(1) *Team selection*: the team should have a mix of talents and include experienced people who are knowledgeable in the process, technology, and application area.

(2) *Team training*: detailed review of the assessment questions; deciding what materials and support tools demonstrate conformance to each question.

(3) *Project preparation*: projects in different stages of development and typical of the standard practice in the organization are chosen by agreement between the team and top management. Representatives of the projects are informed and time allotted in their schedules for the assessment.

(4) *Conduct the assessment*: assessment begins with a briefing explaining the process to the management and project representatives. The assessment team goes through the questionnaire with the project representatives as a group, ensuring consistent interpretation of the questions and obtaining an initial set of answers for each project.

(5) *Draw up results*: a preliminary assessment of the level of maturity is made for each project and for the organization as a whole.

(6) *Discuss results*: the preliminary assessments are discussed. Back-up materials and tool demonstrations are requested to support the affirmative answers that determine the highest likely maturity level (see the section on follow-up questions, below).

(7) *Finalize results*: the organization has the opportunity to discuss the results. A final assessment is given by the team, incorporating the results of the questionnaire, the follow-up questions, and all background evidence.

Note that the above procedure also uses a set of follow-up questions to promote in-depth assessment. These follow-up questions are presented at the end of this appendix.

If you follow the above steps you must be prepared to devote a large amount of effort to the assessment. In return, the insights you gain into your own software development process will be of considerable value.

Making it easy: SEI assessment

Two factors may inhibit you from following the above procedure. Firstly, it may simply be impractical for your organization to allocate the level of resources required for the assessment tasks. Secondly, in the context of the **ami** handbook, it is very difficult to justify a large amount of effort simply as an entry point to defining goals for software measurement.

You will probably want to set a limit on the time and effort devoted to an assessment of no more than two or three days. The results you obtain, therefore, must be interpreted only in very general terms.

Two alternative assessment procedures, neither requiring more than two or three days, are given. Both assume a single assessor is nominated. He or she should be a senior member of staff and experienced in software development. The assessor will go through the assessment questions with representatives of the projects. Time should be allowed for the assessor to review the material, read further background material, and plan the assessment. The time needed should be about two days for review and planning plus two or three days for the assessment.

In self-assessment, there should be someone who checks for evidence that engineering practices are effectively implemented.

Procedure 1

● Review the background material and plan the assessment.

● Concentrate on answers to the Process Metrics and Process Control sections of the questionnaire (between them, they cover 48% of all the questions in the questionnaire).

● Use the follow-up questions to probe all replies to the above two sections, and especially where the assessment questions have a hash sign (#).

● Compile the results, with short general observations, into an assessment report.

Procedure 2

● Review the background material and plan the assessment.

● Concentrate on answers to level 2 (L2) and level 3 (L3) questions (between them they cover 76% of all the questions in the questionnaire).

● Use the follow-up questions to probe replies to the L2 and L3 questions that have a hash sign (#): these cover 28% of all the questions in the questionnaire.

- Compile the results and short general observations into an assessment report. These alternative procedures offer faster, but less consistent, results than the SEI procedure. In the context of the **ami** handbook, the goal-oriented aims of an assessment reduce the risk of these fast-track assessments.

Questionnaire

The questions are divided into seven sections:

(1.1) Organization

(1.2) Resources, Personnel and Training

(1.3) Technology Management

(2.1) Documented Standards and Procedures

(2.2) Process Metrics

(2.3) Data Management and Analysis

(2.4) Process Control

The above sections have retained their original numbers from the SEI questionnaire so that it is easy to cross-reference.

If the motive for assessment is not simply to determine maturity level, the order in which the sections are used can be reviewed. For example, if the objective is to define primary goals for measurement, a more suitable order would be Process Metrics, Process Control, followed by the other sections.

Scoring

The questions are all YES/NO answers and are all assigned to a level. Questions that also have a hash sign (#) are deemed to have a slightly greater importance at their level. Everyone commences at level 1.

To reach level 2, 80% of all questions denoted L2 must have YES answers and 90% of all questions denoted L2 # must have YES answers.

To reach level 3, including the questions from the previous level, 80% of all questions denoted L3 must have YES answers and 90% of all questions denoted L3 # must have YES answers.

To reach levels 4 and 5, the questions from previous levels are again included and the 80% and 90% criteria are again used.

To determine the level of an organization as a whole, the levels of all the organization's projects assessed are averaged.

Terminology

In the questions that follow, certain specific terms are in italics. To improve clarity of the questions, the meaning of these terms is clarified here.

- *Formal Procedure*   A documented series of steps, with guidelines for use.

- *Mechanism*   A means or technique whereby the performance of a task, procedure or process is assured. The mechanism may involve several organizational elements and its documentation may include some combination of function statements, operating plans, position descriptions, and formal procedures. The documentation defines what should be performed, how it should be performed, and who is accountable for the results.

- *Process*   A systematic series of mechanisms, tasks, and procedures directed towards an objective. The software engineering process documentation defines the sequence of steps used to produce a finished product. Each step is described as a task that is carried out using a software engineering methodology or an administrative procedure, and prescribes the automated tools and techniques to be used.

- *Process group*   The software engineering process group is composed of specialists concerned with the software development process used by the organization. Its typical functions include defining and documenting the process, establishing and defining process metrics, support of data gathering and analysis, and advising management on areas requiring further attention. The group typically conducts quarterly management reviews on process status and may provide review leaders.

- *Standard*   An approved, documented, and available set of criteria used to determine the adequacy of an action or object.

Maturity level questions

1.1	**Organization**	
1.1.1	For each project involving software development, is there a designated software manager?	Y / N L2
1.1.2	Does the software manager report directly to the project (or project development) manager?	Y / N L2
1.1.3	Does the Software Quality Assurance (SQA) function have a management reporting channel which is separate from the software development project management?	Y / N # L2
1.1.4	Is there a designated individual or team responsible for the control of software interfaces?	Y / N L3
1.1.5	Is software system engineering represented on the system design team?	Y / N L3
1.1.6	Is there a software configuration control function for each project that involves software development?	Y / N # L2
1.1.7	Is there a software engineering *process group* function?	Y / N # L3
1.2	**Resources, Personnel and Training**	
1.2.1	Does each software developer have a private computer-supported workstation/terminal?	Y / N L3
1.2.2	Is there a required training programme for all newly appointed development managers designed to familiarize them with software project management?	Y / N L2
1.2.3	Is there a required software engineering training programme for software developers?	Y / N # L3
1.2.4	Is there a required software engineering training programme for first-line supervisors of software development?	Y / N L3
1.2.5	Is a formal training programme required for design and code review leaders?	Y / N # L3

1.3   Technology Management

1.3.1   Is a mechanism used for maintaining awareness of the state of the art in software engineering technology?   Y / N   L2

1.3.2   Is a mechanism used for evaluating technologies used by the organization versus those externally available?   Y / N   L3

1.3.3   Is a mechanism used for deciding when to insert new technology into the development process?   Y / N   L4

1.3.4   Is a mechanism used for managing and supporting the introduction of new technologies?   Y / N #   L4

1.3.5   Is a mechanism used for identifying and replacing obsolete technologies?   Y / N #   L5

2.1   Documented Standards and Procedures

2.1.1   Does the software organization use a standardized, documented software development process on each project?   Y / N #   L3

2.1.2   Does the standard software development process documentation describe the use of tools and techniques?   Y / N   L3

2.1.3   Is a formal procedure used in the management review of each software development prior to making contractual commitments?   Y / N #   L2

2.1.4   Is a formal procedure used to assure periodic management review of the status of each software development project?   Y / N   L2

2.1.5   Is there a mechanism for assuring that software subcontractors, if any, follow a disciplined software development process?   Y / N   L2

2.1.6   Are standards used for the content of software development files/folders?   Y / N   L3

2.1.7   For each project, are independent audits conducted for each step of the software development process?   Y / N   L2

2.1.8   Is a mechanism used for assessing existing designs and code for reuse in new applications?   Y / N   L3

2.1.9   Are coding standards applied to each software development project?   Y / N   L2

2.1   **Documented Standards and Procedures (continued)**

2.1.10	Are standards applied to the preparation of unit test cases?	Y / N L3
2.1.11	Are code maintainability standards applied?	Y / N L3
2.1.12	Are internal design review standards applied?	Y / N L4
2.1.13	Are code review standards applied?	Y / N # L4
2.1.14	Is a formal procedure used to make estimates of software size?	Y / N # L2
2.1.15	Is a formal procedure used to produce software development schedules?	Y / N # L2
2.1.16	Are formal procedures applied to estimating software development cost?	Y / N # L2
2.1.17	Is a mechanism used for ensuring that the software design teams understand each software requirement?	Y / N L2
2.1.18	Are man–machine interface standards applied to each appropriate software development project?	Y / N L3

2.2   **Process Metrics**

2.2.1	Are software staffing profiles maintained of actual staffing versus planned staffing?	Y / N L2
2.2.2	Are profiles of software size maintained for each software configuration item, over time?	Y / N # L2
2.2.3	Are statistics of software design errors gathered?	Y / N # L3
2.2.4	Are statistics of software code and test errors gathered?	Y / N # L2
2.2.5	Are design errors projected and compared to actuals?	Y / N # L4
2.2.6	Are code and test errors projected and compared to actuals?	Y / N # L4
2.2.7	Are profiles maintained of actual versus planned software units designed, over time?	Y / N L2

2.2   **Process Metrics (continued)**

2.2.8	Are profiles maintained of actual versus planned software units completing unit testing, over time?	Y / N L2
2.2.9	Are profiles maintained of actual versus planned software units integrated, over time?	Y / N L2
2.2.10	Are target computer memory utilization estimates and actuals tracked?	Y / N L2
2.2.11	Are target computer throughput utilization estimates and actuals tracked?	Y / N L2
2.2.12	Is target computer I/O channel utilization tracked?	Y / N L2
2.2.13	Are design and code review coverages measured and recorded?	Y / N # L4
2.2.14	Is test coverage measured and recorded for each phase of functional testing?	Y / N # L4
2.2.15	Are the action items resulting from design reviews tracked to closure?	Y / N # L3
2.2.16	Are software trouble reports resulting from testing tracked to closure?	Y / N L2
2.2.17	Are the action items resulting from code reviews tracked to closure?	Y / N # L3
2.2.18	Is test progress tracked by deliverable software component and compared to the plan?	Y / N L2
2.2.19	Are profiles maintained of software build/release content versus time?	Y / N L2

2.3   **Data Management and Analysis**

2.3.1	Has a managed and controlled process database been established for process metrics data across all projects?	Y / N # L4
2.3.2	Are the review data gathered during design reviews analysed?	Y / N # L4
2.3.3	Is the error data from code reviews and tests analysed to determine the likely distribution and characteristics of the errors remaining in the product?	Y / N # L4

2.3   Data Management and Analysis (continued)

2.3.4   Are analyses of errors conducted to determine their   Y / N #
          process related causes?   L4

2.3.5   Is a mechanism used for error cause analysis?   Y / N #
                                                                       L5

2.3.6   Are the error causes reviewed to determine the process   Y / N #
          changes required to prevent them?   L5

2.3.7   Is a mechanism used for initiating error prevention   Y / N #
          actions?   L5

2.3.8   Is review efficiency analysed for each project?   Y / N #
                                                                       L4

2.3.9   Is software productivity analysed for major process   Y / N
          steps?   L4

2.4   Process Control

2.4.1   Does senior management have a mechanism for   Y / N #
          regular review of the status of software development   L2
          projects?

2.4.2   Is a mechanism used for periodically assessing the   Y / N #
          software engineering process and implementing   L4
          indicated improvements?

2.4.3   Is a mechanism used for identifying and resolving   Y / N
          system engineering issues that affect software?   L3

2.4.4   Is a mechanism used for independently calling   Y / N
          integration and test issues to the attention of the   L3
          project manager?

2.4.5   Is a mechanism used for regular technical interchanges   Y / N
          with the customer?   L2

2.4.6   Is a mechanism used for ensuring compliance with the   Y / N #
          software engineering standards?   L3

2.4.7   Do software development first-line managers sign off   Y / N #
          on their schedules and cost estimates?   L2

2.4.8   Is a mechanism used for ensuring traceability between   Y / N
          the software requirements and top-level design?   L3

2.4.9   Is a mechanism used for controlling changes to the   Y / N #
          software requirements?   L2

2.4   **Process Control (continued)**

2.4.10	Is there a formal management process for determining if the prototyping of software functions is an appropriate part of the design process?	Y / N L4
2.4.11	Is a mechanism used for ensuring traceability between the software top-level and detailed designs?	Y / N L3
2.4.12	Are internal software design reviews conducted?	Y / N # L3
2.4.13	Is a mechanism used for controlling changes to the software design?	Y / N # L3
2.4.14	Is a mechanism used for ensuring traceability between the software detailed design and the code?	Y / N L3
2.4.15	Are formal records maintained of unit (module) development progress?	Y / N L3
2.4.16	Are software code reviews conducted?	Y / N # L3
2.4.17	Is a mechanism used for controlling changes to the code? (Who can make changes and under what circumstances?)	Y / N # L2
2.4.18	Is a mechanism used for configuration management of the software tools used in the development process?	Y / N L3
2.4.19	Is a mechanism used for verifying that the samples examined by SQA are truly representative of the work performed?	Y / N # L3
2.4.20	Is there a mechanism for assuring that regression testing is routinely performed?	Y / N L2
2.4.21	Is there a mechanism for assuring the adequacy of regression testing?	Y / N # L3
2.4.22	Are formal test case reviews conducted?	Y / N L3

Follow-up questions

Presented here are the follow-up questions of the SEI assessment procedure. Where appropriate, they are used to expand the answers obtained from the SEI questionnaire.

(1)   Where responsibility assignments are being considered, request the name of a specific individual, job title, job description, and evidence of activity, such as monthly reports, meeting reports, control logs.

(2)   Where the existence of a group is being considered, request names of members, the organization represented, and recent meeting agendas and minutes.

(3)   Where the existence of education or training programmes is being considered, request the schedule of recent courses offered, course outlines, names of attendees, and qualifications of instructors and students.

(4)   Where the existence of a mechanism, procedure, standard, criterion or guideline is being considered, request a copy of the controlling document, its revision history, the name of individuals responsible for tracking, job descriptions, and recent issue/activity reports.

(5)   Where the use of profiles, tracking reports, planned vs actual comparisons, and measurements are being considered, request the three most recent reports, measurement summaries or comparisons.

(6)   Where computations or analysis of data is being considered, request copies of the most recent computations, analysis reports or summaries showing results or conclusions reached.

(7)   Where the initiation of actions is being considered, request copies of recent action tracking and/or summary reports.

(8)   Where the conduct of certain actions or use of facilities is being considered, request evidence in the form of procedures, responsibilities or tracking systems to demonstrate performance.

(9)   Where the existence of a facility, capability, practice or method is being considered, request supporting evidence in the form of inventory lists, tracking and usage reports, instruction manuals, education programmes, etc.

(10) Where the use of an automated tool or facility is being considered, request a demonstration of that tool or facility.

Examples of Goals and Metrics

Examples of Goals and Metrics

Tables A2.1 to A2.9 contain some example goals and related metrics to help you identify goals and metrics for your measurement programme. We do not claim that these tables are anywhere near complete or exhaustive. The first table gives an example goal tree to show how goals are associated with two levels of sub-goals. The metrics associated with each sub-goal are given in the tables which follow. There is a table for each sub-goal. Each table gives a list of metrics which could be collected to support the goal. You should note that it is not necessary to collect all the metrics in the list.

Subjective metrics are indicated in bold type.

Table A2.1 An example goal tree.

Primary goals	Sub-goals level 1	Sub-goals level 2

To support project management with process data	Control effort of each phase
	   Control testing
	   Control remake
	Estimate cost
	   Analyse methods
		Control specification
		Control design
		
		Control reusability and
		tools support

To support project management with process and product data	Control productivity
	   Analyse product complexity
	   Analyse volumes
	   Analyse resource consumption
	Control effort of each phase
	   Control testing
	   Control rework
	Estimate cost
	   Analyse methods
		Control effort
		
		Control specification
		Control design
		
		Control reusability
		and tools support

To attain an error rate of x errors per 1000 LOC	Control testing effort Control reliability and location Control conformity to requirements Improve quality assurance	Analyse testing effort Analyse test coverage Analyse errors found Analyse errors found through QA

To reduce rework time to x% of the development time	Control maintainability
	   Control effort to fix bugs
	Improve productivity
	   Control bottlenecks
	Improve quality assurance
		Analyse code structure
		Analyse complexity
		Analyse human factors
		
		Analyse defects found

To control the introduction of a new technology	Control productivity
	   Analyse product complexity
	   Analyse volumes
	   Analyse resources consumption
	Control maintainability
	   Control effort to fix bugs
		Control effort
		
		Analyse code structure
		Analyse complexity

Table A2.2 Control effort of each phase.

Control specification	Number of sub-systems Number of functions Number of specification hours
Control design	Number of data sets Number of interfaces Number of units Number of I/O variables Number of design hours
Control testing	Number of testing hours
Control rework	Number of non-conformances to requirements Number of design changes Number of hours to correct problems

Table A2.3 Control cost.

Control cost	Actual cost of each project phase Estimated cost for each phase
Control reusability	Number of new units Number of modified units Number of reused units Delivered lines of code (per new/modified/reused unit) Developed lines of code (SLOCs) Number of documents pages
Analyse methods and tools support	Number of computer hours **Adequacy of methods** **Adequacy of tools** Number of bugs observed in tools

Table A2.4 Control maintainability.

Analyse code structure	Number of decisions/unit Number of I/O variables/unit Number of calls from a given module
Analyse complexity	Number of documents pages **Evaluate complexity/unit**
Control effort to fix bugs	Number of hours for correction Number of errors corrected Number of units modified Number of errors detected during system/ integration tests

Table A2.5 Control productivity.

Control effort	Number of hours/development phase Number of weeks elapsed
Analyse product complexity	**Evaluate complexity/unit**
Analyse volumes	Number of units (new/reused/modified) Delivered lines of code
Analyse resources consumption	Number of computer hours Number of person working/category/ development phase

Table A2.6 Control testing effort.

Analyse testing effort	Number of testing hours Number of test data sets
Analyse test coverage	Inter-module test coverage

Table A2.7 Control reliability.

Analyse errors found and localization	Number of design changes Number of non-conformances to standards Number of failures detected
Control conformity to requirements	Number of non-conformances to requirements Percentage of requirements traceable

Table A2.8 Improve quality assurance.

Analyse errors found through QA	Number of failures detected through QA activities
	Origin of these errors
	Number of QA hours
	Number of document pages

Table A2.9 Improve productivity.

Analyse human factors	Number of delivered source lines of code (SLOC) / person involved
	Number of detected errors/unit
	Number of requirements traceable to design and code
	Percentage of tasks supported by tools
Control bottlenecks	Number of computer hours/person
	Percentage of wasted time and origin

Basic Metrics Set

This section has been completed with the support of the **ami** validation projects. Metrics are related to :

- Resources
  - Project development effort
  - Resource usage
  - Staffing profiles

- Process
  - Project development time
  - Slippage
  - Cost of non-quality
  - Maturity level
  - Project type
  - Number of changes
  - Number of failures
  - Number of process faults
  - Test coverage

- Product
  - Source code size
  - System size
  - Number of document pages
  - Cyclomatic number
  - Structure metric
  - Number of product faults

In the following pages, each metric presentation uses the template defined for Step 7 of the **ami** method.

- Metric
  - A2 DEFINITION
  - A3 GOALS
  - A4 ANALYSIS PROCEDURE
  - A5 RESPONSIBILITIES FOR ANALYSIS

- Primitives
  - B2 DEFINITION
  - B3 COLLECTION PROCEDURE
  - B4 RESPONSIBILITIES FOR COLLECTION

Resources

A1   NAME
Project development effort

A2   DEFINITION

Project development effort is the total time expended in a process on a product. It is collected for each activity of development (specification, design, implementation, testing, installation), and as a total for the project duration.

A3   GOALS

It is an input to cost control and prediction, and is a key indicator of progress. It is also used for assessing the impact of new technology and modelling productivity.

A4   ANALYSIS PROCEDURE

Effort data is compared to past project data and to estimates. If more effort is required to complete a phase than was planned, it is likely that the remaining phases will require proportionally more effort as well. Deviation in effort expenditure can also signal the presence of quality problems.

A5   RESPONSIBILITIES FOR ANALYSIS

The project manager should analyse the data at project milestones. Software departments should review costs on a regular basis and at project completion.

B2   PRIMITIVES DEFINITION

Monthly effort spent on each cost category identified as suitable for knowledge and control.

B3   COLLECTION PROCEDURE

Time sheet.

B4   RESPONSIBILITIES FOR COLLECTION

Team members are responsible for correctly recording time spent on different cost categories and for filling in time sheets on time.

A1 NAME

Resource usage

A2 DEFINITION

Resource usage is represented by various numbers characterizing the development environment, e.g. CPU time, number of terminals used, number of graphical terminals used, number of software licences. All these characteristics should reflect the environment and process phase.

A3 GOALS

Often used as a measure of development activity. Also used to predict investment costs for process improvement. Related costs must be integrated into project cost modelling.

A4 ANALYSIS PROCEDURE

CPU hours or number of terminals used increasing too early or too late might be caused by staffing problems or overlap of design and coding phases.

A5 RESPONSIBILITIES FOR ANALYSIS

Project manager should evaluate resource usage as should department managers who are responsible for investment decisions.

B2 PRIMITIVES DEFINITION

Number of terminals
Number of software licences
CPU time, disk access

B3 COLLECTION PROCEDURE

Number of terminals or licences can be counted manually. CPU time can be measured by tools delivered with most operating systems.

B4 RESPONSIBILITIES FOR COLLECTION

Support engineers should regularly monitor usage of the installation for which they are responsible and circulate this information to the project managers.

A1 NAME
Staffing profiles

A2 DEFINITION
Staffing profiles is a qualitative (subjective) metric to characterize team size over time.

A3 GOALS
Prediction of cost and project time-scales. Evaluation of process capability and productivity.

A4 ANALYSIS PROCEDURE
The actual profile is plotted on an x-t plot with the predicted project values.

A5 RESPONSIBILITIES FOR ANALYSIS
Project manager and team leaders.

B2 PRIMITIVES DEFINITION
A straight count of the number of engineers at a given point in time.

B3 COLLECTION PROCEDURE
The count will be collected at specific intervals, e.g. weekly or monthly.

B4 RESPONSIBILITIES FOR COLLECTION
Project managers should collect this data.

Process

A1 NAME

Project development time

A2 DEFINITION

Development time is defined as the elapsed time, in weeks, for each phase (milestone) and for the total project duration.

A3 GOALS

Improve project estimates. Process improvement by detection of bottlenecks. Early detection of project overruns.

A4 ANALYSIS PROCEDURE

Project development time is compared to estimates and to past project data. Project development time of phases is analysed to provide historical values for the relative sizes of the phases.

A5 RESPONSIBILITIES FOR ANALYSIS

Project manager and team leaders should analyse the data at each milestone. Historical data should be accumulated at the departmental or company level.

B2 PRIMITIVES DEFINITION

Phase time is the elapsed time in weeks.

B3 COLLECTION PROCEDURE

Project managers agree milestone completion dates, which are then entered into a project management system.

B4 RESPONSIBILITIES FOR COLLECTION

Project managers are responsible for maintaining updated lists of phase times. The departmental or company Quality Manager will keep an historical database of the phase times for past projects.

A1 NAME
Slippage

A2 DEFINITION
Slippage is the difference of the old estimates to new estimates.

A3 GOALS
Control of project schedules and resources.

A4 ANALYSIS PROCEDURE
Slippage is a key indicator of problems in the process. Non- existence of slippage data shows problems in project management, as does regular and uncorrected slippage.

A5 RESPONSIBILITIES FOR ANALYSIS
Project managers and team leaders should analyse slippage data at regular intervals, e.g. weekly or monthly.

B2 PRIMITIVES DEFINITION
Estimates and re-estimates of project costs and schedules. Actual costs and duration.

B3 COLLECTION PROCEDURE
At predefined time intervals, evaluation of the remaining work to complete the current phase and the subsequent ones has to be conducted. Remaining work might be expressed in terms of effort, time or cost. Estimates are needed for each module and for the total.

B4 RESPONSIBILITIES FOR COLLECTION
It is important that those most closely involved in the work (i.e. team members) give estimates and measures. Consolidation is achieved by the project manager.

A1   NAME

Cost of non-quality

A2   DEFINITION

Cost of non-quality is the cost generated by non-conformance to customer or company requirements when working on any document or product.

A3   GOALS

Used for process improvement.

A4   ANALYSIS PROCEDURE

Comparison of cost of non-quality to development cost indicates areas for improvement. Trends show success or failure of improvement actions.

A5   RESPONSIBILITIES FOR ANALYSIS

Project managers and quality engineers should collectively analyse the data.

B2   PRIMITIVES DEFINITION

Rework effort, cost of quality assurance, cost of testing, cost of corrective maintenance after project end. These are measured in man-hours.

B   COLLECTION PROCEDURE

Data is collected from time sheets at the completion of a phase or maintenance job. An improved procedure may need to be put in place to be able to identify these costs separately.

B4   RESPONSIBILITIES FOR COLLECTION

Quality engineers, team leaders and project managers.

A1   NAME

Maturity level

A2   DEFINITION

Maturity level is a subjective metric that characterizes the control and understanding of the software process.

A3   GOALS

Quality and productivity improvement. Process improvement.

A4   ANALYSIS PROCEDURE

Maturity level scores should be analysed by area (organization, documentation) and compared to company strategy in each area.

A5   RESPONSIBILITIES FOR ANALYSIS

Department and project managers.

B2   PRIMITIVES DEFINITION

See Appendix 1.

A1   NAME

Project type

A2   DEFINITION

Project type is an attribute defining the external constraints on the development process of the project and on the usage of the final product.

A3   GOALS

Cost and productivity modelling. Quality evaluation.

A4   ANALYSIS PROCEDURE

The attributes are calibrated to project cost and schedules.

A5   RESPONSIBILITIES FOR ANALYSIS

Project managers and quality engineers.

B2   PRIMITIVES DEFINITION

Project characteristics, e.g. customer ype; target system type; reliability requirement, etc.

Project attributes which are the attributes of the project which are required to calibrate the cost model.

B3   COLLECTION PROCEDURE

Estimates are done at the beginning of the projects and measures are collected at the end of the main milestones.

B4   RESPONSIBILITIES FOR COLLECTION

Project managers.

A1 NAME

Number of changes

A2 DEFINITION

Number of change requests committed to be implemented.

A3 GOALS

Project monitoring. Often used as explanatory variables for development effort justification or reliability evaluation.

A4 ANALYSIS PROCEDURE

Change rate is a key indicator of the software development process quality and project requirement stability. Correlated to failures observed, project slippage and productivity.

A very high change rate should spur investigation and support decision for auditing the development process, product and organization.

A5 RESPONSIBILITIES FOR ANALYSIS

Team leaders, quality engineers and managers.

B2 PRIMITIVES DEFINITION

Number of changes requested at monthly intervals, number of changes implemented, type of change, fault correction, new function, requirements change, performance improvement.

B3 COLLECTION PROCEDURE

Change requests are counted at regular intervals. Additional information is exploited.

B4 RESPONSIBILITIES FOR COLLECTION

Data should be collected by the person responsible for change control.

A1 NAME

Number of failures

A2 DEFINITION

Number of failures is the number of software behaviour discrepancies. The program has to be executing for a failure to occur. It can include deficiencies in performance or response time.

A3 GOALS

Quality control. Used in quality and reliability modelling.

A4 ANALYSIS PROCEDURE

Correlated to test coverage measurement, size of code, development effort. Trends in failure detection and correction are extrapolated to predict project completion or product quality.

A5 RESPONSIBILITIES FOR ANALYSIS

Quality engineer, project manager.

B2 PRIMITIVES DEFINITION

Number of test failure reports during testing phase. Number of customer failure reports.

B3 COLLECTION PROCEDURE

Generally, failure observations are reported in test or validation results or change requests. These are counted at regular intervals.

B4 RESPONSIBILITIES FOR COLLECTION

Test engineers, project managers.

A1 NAME

Number of process faults

A2 DEFINITION

Number of faults detected that are manifested by corrections and modifications.

A3 GOALS

Process improvement and quality control.

A4 ANALYSIS PROCEDURE

Relatively high levels in faults detected indicate areas for process improvements. Examples are:

- large number of coding errors indicate unstructured code.
- large number of specifications errors indicate either lack of applications experience or an inappropriate life cycle.

Large time gaps between process fault occurrence and detection indicate areas for improved reviewing and testing.

A5 RESPONSIBILITIES FOR ANALYSIS

Quality engineers, project manager.

B2 PRIMITIVES DEFINITION

Process phase (document) that is implicated in the modification. Where observed – review/inspection, testing; nature – specification missing, clerical error, technical problem.

B3 COLLECTION PROCEDURE

All corrections have to be diagnosed to identify the process which is the source of the problem. The data is then counted at regular intervals or at project end.

B4 RESPONSIBILITIES FOR COLLECTION

Engineers that implement changes have to give the diagnosis. The project manager is responsible for aggregating data.

A1   NAME

Test coverage

A2   DEFINITION

Test coverage is a ratio that indicates the extent to which software is tested. All types of testing strategies are included, i.e. unit tests, integration tests, systems test.

A3   GOALS

Establish a minimum test criterion. Monitoring test progress. Might be compared to reliability evaluation results to support testing strategy selection.

A4   ANALYSIS PROCEDURE

Compared to testing effort and number of failures observed. Testing effort and coverage should grow simultaneously.

If testing coverage is high and the number of failures low, the product quality should be high. The optimum test strategy at any point is the one that yields the greatest reduction in operational failure 'cost'. Hence, the optimum average test strategy will be to select input data in a way that will reduce failure intensity most rapidly with respect to execution time.

A5   RESPONSIBILITIES FOR ANALYSIS

Team leader and test engineers.

B2   PRIMITIVES DEFINITION

Number of instructions executed, number of instructions, number of branches executed, number of branches, number of linear code sequence and jump (LCSAJ) executed, number of linear code sequence and jump (LCSAJ).

B3   COLLECTION PROCEDURE

Dynamic analysis tools are needed to trace the testing process.

B4   RESPONSIBILITIES FOR COLLECTION

Testing engineer. Collated by the project manager.

Product

A   NAME

Source code size

A2   DEFINITION

A static measure of the number of lines of code (SLOC) that are developed and those that are delivered.

A3   GOALS

Used in productivity models. Used in reliability models, cost modelling and planning. Source code growth rate is a strong progress indicator during implementation and key stability indicator during the testing phases.

A4   ANALYSIS PROCEDURE

Source code size is directly compared to development effort. The growth of source code closely reflects requirements completeness and the software development process. A deviation from the growth model indicates that the project is deviating from the plan.

A5   RESPONSIBILITIES FOR ANALYSIS

Team leaders and project managers.

B2   PRIMITIVES DEFINITION

Code is classified by:

(1) new, modified and reused;

(2) module, and total;

(3) delivered SLOC, developed SLOC, delivered source instructions.

The definition of what is included and what is excluded as a line of source code (SLOC) will vary from one environment to another. A clear and precise definition must be obtained for each environment and each software language used.

B3   COLLECTION PROCEDURE

Can be collected by an in-house collection tool or via compilers.

B4   RESPONSIBILITIES FOR COLLECTION

Team leaders should keep up-to-date data of their projects.

A1 NAME

System size

A2 DEFINITION

System size is a direct count of the number of characteristic units selected to estimate the volume of work, e.g. function points, statements, lines of code, number of objects.

A3 GOALS

Prediction of the amount of work, product size – estimation. Regular estimates constitute a key indicator of requirements stability and completeness.

A4 ANALYSIS PROCEDURE

System size is often compared to development effort and development time. In order to perform valid estimations, the system is usually broken down into sub-systems (system sub-part for which complete requirements might be written) and even smaller units. The more breakdown achieved, the more reliable the estimation will be. Undefined or incomplete parts are to be identified and isolated.

A5 RESPONSIBILITIES

Project manager.

B2 PRIMITIVES DEFINITION

Number of functions, number of data inputs and outputs, number of files, number of screens, number of parameters, number of function points.

B3 COLLECTION PROCEDURE

Specification and design documents are analysed to count the number of elements.

B4 RESPONSIBILITIES FOR COLLECTION

Team leaders.

A1　NAME

Number of document pages

A2　DEFINITION

The total number of pages of documentation associated with a software product.

A3　GOALS

Product sizing, visibility and traceability control.

A4　ANALYSIS PROCEDURE

Size of documentation is often compared to effort data, project type, lines of code or system size. Document size growth is an indication of phase progress.

A5　RESPONSIBILITIES FOR ANALYSIS

Team leader and quality engineer.

B2　PRIMITIVES DEFINITION

Number of pages and number of diagrams for each document.

B3　COLLECTION PROCEDURE

Most word processing systems can count total number of document pages. This data should be collected at document release

B4　RESPONSIBILITIES FOR COLLECTION

Quality engineer.

A1   NAME
Cyclomatic number

A2   DEFINITION
The number of linearly independent paths through a program.

A3   GOALS
Testability/test completion criteria, complexity prediction, test coverage, quality analysis.

A4   ANALYSIS PROCEDURE
This has been shown to be associated with error rates. It is usually collected via static analysis tools and code instrumentation. Modules with large values of cyclomatic number (>10) are identified for quality control.

A5   RESPONSIBILITIES
Programmer, team member.

B2   PRIMITIVES DEFINITION
Number of nodes and edges in the source program's control flow graph.

B3   COLLECTION PROCEDURE
Static analysis tools are used to produce a control flow graph and to count the primitives.

B4   RESPONSIBILITIES FOR COLLECTION
Software engineers should analyse their own code as soon as code is written. Data is then passed on to quality engineers.

A1 NAME

Structure metric

A2 DEFINITION

Number of units in the structure of the source code or other formal structure such as an SADT model.

A3 GOALS

Often used as a measure of complexity. Can be used for estimation of development effort, measurement of maintainability, identification of critical points for allocation of effective quality assurance, measurement of productivity.

A4 ANALYSIS PROCEDURE

Correlated with source code size, failure rate, development effort.

A5 RESPONSIBILITIES FOR ANALYSIS

Team leaders and quality engineers.

B2 PRIMITIVES DEFINITION

Data flow complexity, number of data structures from which the module retrieves data, number of data structures that the module updates, number of data flows into a module, number of data flows from a module.

B3 COLLECTION PROCEDURE

Specification and design documents are analysed to produce the counts.

B4 RESPONSIBILITIES FOR COLLECTION

Team members.

A1 NAME
Number of product faults

A2 DEFINITION
Number of product faults resulting in a failure.

A3 GOALS
Often used as system acceptance criteria; used in quality and reliability modelling (product fault rate) and in process improvement.

A4 ANALYSIS PROCEDURE
Correlated to test coverage measurement, size of code, development effort. Product fault rate should continually decrease in subsequent phases (i.e. cut by 50% each phase). If fault rate is low and the detection rate does not decline from phase to phase, inadequate testing and a less reliable system are likely. Track product faults vs total estimated size of project (in SLOC). Product faults decline as the software development process and technology improve.

A5 RESPONSIBILITIES FOR ANALYSIS
Quality engineer, team leaders.

B2 PRIMITIVES DEFINITION
Count number of faults classified as one of component missing, component incorrect, clerical error, combinatorial, coding error etc. Number of components affected, gravity (as observed consequences), number of other modules modified at the same time.

B3 COLLECTION PROCEDURE
Faults are counted at each implementation of a change request.

B4 RESPONSIBILITIES FOR COLLECTION
Development engineers.

Further Case Studies

Here are three case studies that show further and different applications of the **ami** method. The first shows that metrics can flag up problems early in the measurement programme, the second demonstrates the use of metrics in improving the testing process and the third gives a larger example of a goal tree.

Example 1

The company that is the subject of this case study is a major supplier of airborne equipment, most of which involves the use of embedded computers and software. The project we shall consider was a safety-critical application.

The need for a measurement programme was identified by the senior management of the software engineering department and by the technical management of the division. The **ami** method was identified as the best way to implement their measurement programme. This case study describes the experience from the first project that was implemented using the **ami** method. It was the first project from which a coherent set of metrics was gathered and formed the baseline against which to measure further improvements in the future and as an aid to further enhancing their development process.

The user problem

All the costs of the products and processes of their developments were closely monitored. Over a four-year period the cost of each development phase and the cost of each deliverable document had been monitored and analysed on all projects. This had allowed them to assess whether their development procedures were adequate and to provide more accurate estimates for future projects. This analysis was mainly subjective but did enable them to identify some improvements to their development process. However, they had reached the stage where further progress could only be made by measuring more detailed attributes of their process. The cost data had shown that the hardware–software integration phase constituted a very high proportion of the total cost of the project and it was in this area that the company decided to concentrate its efforts.

They realized that before they could consider any more improvements to their process they would have to gain a more detailed knowledge of their present position. With this in mind the initial

Example 1

objective was to generate goals and metrics to provide an assessment of the present software production process with the focus on the integration process. Later, they would be able to measure the effect of any changes to the integration process.

As a secondary goal they had not measured the impact of new tools upon the effectiveness of their development process. They decided to include an assessment of the effectiveness of a code analyser tool in their measurement programme. There was a doubt that many new tools offer little or no benefit and may actually be counter-productive. Using the measurement programme they could measure the tools' effectiveness on their process to determine if they were in fact achieving any tangible benefits.

The solution used

In analysing the development environment they made use of the life-cycle model in DOD2167A (1988). This gave them a very comprehensive set of products and processes with very little effort and provided a basis for the analysis of the goals. Only minor problems were experienced in goal analysis but nothing serious. In general, the production of goals, sub-goals and metrics was found to be straightforward with no major problems. All the information from this activity was summarized in the metrics plan and was used as a reference to all interested parties and as a guide to the metrication activities.

It was initially decided that data collection would use manual methods. This was mainly using forms and manual counting. However, after a short time the quantity of data being produced far exceeded their initial estimates. They found it necessary to automate the analysis process; the final amount of data was over seven times that estimated. Data collection remained manual but the information received was entered into a spreadsheet package to provide rapid and efficient processing and analysis. To further support the analysis process, a small program was written to perform various searches on the data received.

Goals

As a result of applying the **ami** method the following long-term goals and sub-goals were identified.

Goal 1: To improve the development process

Within this the following sub-goals were identified.

1.1   To reduce the present rework levels by 20%.

1.2   To reduce the percentage of errors produced overall by 30%.

1.3   To reduce the percentage of errors found after unit test by 20%.

1.4   To improve the estimates of the time to complete the project.

It should be noted that at this point in their measurement programme they were establishing baselines against which to measure improvements. The initial thrust of the measurements taken would be to establish the present levels against which the percentage improvements could be measured.

Goal 2: To measure the effectiveness of a new code analyser tool

At the start of the measurement programme the company had no quantitative data on the contribution that tools were making to effectiveness of the development process. It was decided to measure the effectiveness of a code analysis tool as a starting point.

2.1   Measure the time spent during testing using the code analysis tool.

2.2   Measure the number of code changes due to using the code analysis tool.

Metrics used

Since this was their initial usage of the **ami** method, the company kept the metric set simple.

M.1   *Integration time used*: The number of modules integrated against the cumulative effort expended.

M.2   *Module stability*: The number of defects discovered in integration.

M.3   *Problem cause identification*: The number of defects detected for each type.

M.4   *Tool code changes*: The number of modifications made to the code due to shortcomings identified by the code analysis tool.

M.5   *Tool effort use*: The number of modules tested using the code analysis tool against cumulative effort.

Metrics M.1 and M.5 proved problematic since the company's

Example 1

configuration management system could not identify at any given moment how many modules had been analysed using the code analysis tool. This shortcoming in their configuration management has since been rectified. The other metrics worked as intended.

Analysis of the results

The information obtained from the initial metric set was used to set up a baseline against which the performance of subsequent projects can be measured. However, there were some immediate benefits.

The first was from the analysis of rework and modification causes, which highlighted two areas that had the effect of increasing the level of rework needing to be carried out on the project. These were the large number of requirement changes that had arrived very late in the life cycle and the large number of late hardware changes. These two causes were identified to give rise to a disproportionately large amount of rework.

The second was the measured benefit obtained from the code analysis tool. They discovered that the tool reported very few genuine errors for the amount of time expended on using it. They concluded that virtually any other testing strategy would have revealed at least as many if not more defects for the level of effort devoted to the use of the tool.

Benefits

Within the division which used the **ami** method, a number of immediate benefits were obtained. The main aim of the initial application of the **ami** method was to establish a baseline against which improvements could be assessed. This was achieved and would be used to measure the performance of subsequent projects. In the short term the measurement highlighted some immediate improvement areas. These were:

- the large number of software updates that were being carried out late in the software life cycle;

- the number of modifications that were arising from unexpected sources, e.g. requirements and hardware changes, late in the project;

- the small benefit that is provided by the code analysis tool in relation to the level of effort needed for its effective use.

Costs

The cost overhead of applying the **ami** method was very small at a few per cent of the software development costs. This was the initial application of the method and so it was kept deliberately simple. The company currently has plans to implement a more ambitious metric set in its next project.

Conclusions

The company concluded from its initial application of the method that the method was usable and easy to apply. The method was easily understood with only a small amount of study.

This case study shows that even just putting in a metrics programme can highlight problems in your process. Once discovered, a lot of these problems seem obvious and are often easily fixed. It is these problems that will give you highly cost effective improvements.

One thing that this case highlights is that having concrete figures helps convince management of a course of action. In this case they were able to show documented evidence of the repercussions of allowing requirements changes late into the development cycle. Management can then weigh the advantages and disadvantages of allowing requirements changes in the future.

Example 2

This example is based on the experience of a large European telecommunications equipment manufacturer. The company was aware of the trend of their business to become more software-intensive. Today, the software development cost of a new switching system is up to 80% of the total development costs.

The project used in this case study was a very large telecommunications system consisting of over a million lines of software. It was being developed in a distributed environment in centres based in four European countries. The system was developed on IBM mainframes but targeted on different hardware.

Example 2

Problem description

The main objective of the measurement programme was to gain better control of the software and its development process. This meant initially to gain an understanding of the process and the products and their characteristics. A short-term objective was to help achieve the next delivery milestone. Longer term they had the objective of improving their development process and applying the lessons to the next generation of products.

Approach used

The SEI Capability Maturity Model was used for an initial assessment of the environment. The top level goals were identified and the metrics derived via sub-goals. A metrics plan was developed to support the data collection process.

One of their goals was to improve their module test strategy. They applied a method of scheduling modules for module testing based on measuring module complexity. It was based on the correlation of complexity and error levels, i.e. complex modules tend to have more errors associated with them. Thus, their strategy was to put the more complex modules earlier in the test schedule. The project was looking to clear as many errors as possible early in the testing process and to leave the easy modules till later.

Two sorts of metric were collected:

(1)   Static product metrics based on the complexity measures of the code calculated using the COSMOS tool.

(2)   *A postiori* data consisting of:

(a)   process metrics extracted from their configuration management system, e.g. number of changes or error reports;

(b)   subjective estimates by the designers.

The results of applying this technique are given in Figure A4.1. It shows the rate at which errors are detected as a percentage of the total number of errors detected during module testing. The top line gives the best theoretical rate at which errors can be detected and the lower line the worst. The middle lines indicate the rate using the complexity measure and without. The results show a distinct improvement in the rate at which errors are detected.

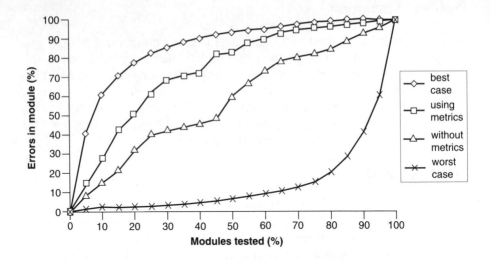

Figure A4.1 Module error detection rates.

Goals

The main goal for their measurement programme was:

● to improve the testing activities for the current release of the system.

This was decomposed into two sub-goals:

G1.1 To get better resource estimates for the testing phase.

G1.2 To apply better testing strategy.

Benefits

The benefits perceived by the company include having greater confidence in producing a new product release with a higher level of quality. They also believe they now have the complexity of their product under control.

Conclusion

This example shows the **ami** method being used to:

(1) dynamically improve the development process;

(2) measure and verify the improvement.

Example 3

The company believes that the **ami** method offers them a consistent and general framework to support their measurement programme objectives.

Example 3

Background

This case study comes from the software development branch of a large European computer manufacturer. The company had some experience of collecting metrics but did not have a method to undertake a large-scale measurement programme. They selected the **ami** method since they perceived that it would increase the visibility of their software development process and would help to measure and improve their product.

They started by applying the **ami** method to three of their projects which were using COBOL: a new development of about 44 man-months, and two maintenance projects of 120 and 50 man- months.

Problem description

The company's target was to produce a product which met its customers' requirements while delivering it within the deadlines and budget constraints. From this they targeted cost prediction, project scheduling, quality management and quality measurement as key areas.

Approach used

This company did not use the SEI Capability Maturity Model at the start of the programme. Instead they used their customer requirements to help them focus on the key areas. However, they were not sufficiently thorough in validating their goals at this stage which led to some problems later in the programme.

The basic metric set in the **ami** handbook was used to help identify the metrics to be applied. They also used their earlier experience of collecting metrics to help identify the more cost-effective metrics.

When they produced the metrics plan they found that it was very large (about 120 pages). The structure was modified to shorten it and made easier to update and evolve with their programme.

A program was written to help collect some of the metrics. The rest were collected using forms. A spreadsheet was used to analyse the data and help produce graphical presentations of the data and metrics.

The selection of a presentation of the results was found to need some thought but eventually a tabular presentation was found that worked.

Goals and metrics used

The main goal was:

- To improve productivity while maintaining quality.

In order to make this more manageable the goal was broken down into sub-goals.

- Sub-goal 1: Evaluate productivity
- Sub-goal 2: Monitor quality
- Sub-goal 3: Detect impediments to higher productivity

The following tables give the metrics linked to each sub-goal and the questions used to derive the metrics. Each table consist of a sub-goal with a list of associated questions and the respective metrics. Subjective metrics are indicated in italic type.

G1 Sub-goal 1: Evaluate productivity

Q1. What is the productivity for completed projects?

Metrics:
Effort expended per project
Number of new source code instructions per project

Q2. What is the size of the developed system/software unit?

Metrics:
Number of major functions
Number of data sets
Number of units
Number of lines of code developed
Total number of lines of code
Number of lines of comment

Example 3

Number of lines of data division
Number of lines of procedure division
Subjective input data for function point calculation
Number of pages of documentation

Q3. What is the level of change (i.e. the proportion of new and modified modules to unchanged units)?
Metrics:
Number of new units
Number of modified units
Number of reused units
Number of unchanged units
Number of deleted units
Complete unit tests

Q4. What is the complexity of the application?
Metrics:
Number of data sets
Number of calls
Number of input/output variables
Complexity rating (by team leaders)

Q5. In which programming language is the component or system written?
Metrics:
Complete module list

Q6. How much documentation is there?

Metrics:
Number of pages of documentation

Q7. What is the effort spent in the development?

Metrics:
Number of specification hours
Number of coding hours
Number of testing hours

G1 Sub-goal 2: Monitor quality

Q1. How many residual errors are still in the system on delivery?

Metrics:
Number of errors detected during use
Seriousness of each error detected
Intermodule test coverage (unit test)

Q2. What is the quality of the documentation delivered?

Metrics:
Number of documents delivered
Number of documents reviewed
Number of documents conforming to standard
Rating of document quality
Evaluation of the final quality assurance report

Q3. What is the quality of the documentation for post delivery support?

Metrics:
Number of documents used for support
Number of documents reviewed
Number of documents conforming to the company standard
Rating of document quality
Evaluation of the final quality assurance report

Q4. Are there structural deficiencies in the software?

Metrics:
Number of calls
Number of input/output calls
Number of decisions per unit
Evaluation of the final quality assurance report

Example 3

G1 Sub-goal 3: Detect impediments to higher productivity

Q1. Are errors found in time? When and by what activity were they found?

Metrics:
Number of errors found in time (i.e. detected in the same phase as they were introduced)
Number of errors not found in time
Evaluation of the final quality assurance report

Q2. Are there resource bottlenecks?

Metrics:
Origin of bottlenecks
Number of computer hours used per person
Proportion of wasted hours and reason

Q3. Is there sufficient exploitation of reuse?

Metrics:
Evaluation of the final quality assurance report

Q4. What are the problem modules and problem causes?

Metrics:
Number of faults per unit
Unit size
Unit identifier
Proportion of faults by category per unit

Benefits

The company perceived that it benefited directly by getting increased visibility of its development process, improved cost estimates and insights into better software management.

An indirect benefit was that the measurement programme contributed to them obtaining their ISO 9001 certification.

Costs

The first project to which the company applied **ami** required about 6–7% of the whole project effort. This included the installation of the metrics tool and familiarization with MS EXCEL. In the subsequent projects this decreased to 2%. They expect to bring this to below 1% in future projects.

Conclusion

The company concluded that the **ami** method made them think in a top-down way and proceed from strategic objectives to more concrete aims. In the early stages they were very enthusiastic and used many goals. The **ami** method showed that the goals they had used to derive metrics were at too high a level and needed more careful analysis. This included identifying more knowledge goals.

The **ami** method has given them the experience and confidence to continue to extend and expand their metrics.

Glossary of Terms

ami   As in **ami** ESPRIT project and **ami** consortium, **ami** approach, **ami** method, and **ami** validation projects. Acronym for Application of Metrics in Industry and for Assess, Analyse, Metricate, Improve.

Analysis   As in analysis of primary goals to derive sub-goals and then metrics and as in analysis of measurement data to control and improve software development. **ami** stresses the importance of performing the analysis within the context of an organization's development process, i.e. identifying participants when deriving metrics who then interpret the data using their background knowledge of the situation.

Assessment   The general activity of looking at software development or the business environment and assessing what are the important issues. This helps to define valid primary goals, i.e. goals relevant to the software development environment in which software development is taking place, that give significant leverage without being too ambitious. This has a more specific meaning when used in the SEI assessment procedure.

Attribute   A feature or characteristic of an entity which can usually be measured directly.

Capability Maturity Model   The model defines a set of key practice activities that constitute good software engineering practice. The different key areas are rated as more or less critical for achieving quality software and for reducing risks. The criticality of the key areas is used to define a maturity scale against which projects and organizations can be classified. The model is developed by the Software Engineering Institute (SEI).

Communications diagram   A drawing representing flow of information between people in a work environment. It can be used at various stages of the **ami** method to check the suitability of selected goals and metrics in terms of the information flow within the current environment and to help identify problems that might arise later.

Control and improvement   The basic objective of the **ami** approach is to support short-term control and long-term improvement in software development. Emphasis is on achieving this control through better understanding and planning (of both project schedules and project quality) and of problems (risk management).

Data   As in collected data and derived measurement data. The collected data is the numbers that result from the counting (or subjective evaluation) procedure and the relevant entity identifiers. These are processed if necessary to derive the measurement data that constitute the metrics. Alternative terms are values and (sometimes) measures.

Entity   Literally 'thing', product or activity. In the book entities are classified as resource, process or product entities. The book concentrates on the development process, but other important process entities are the software end-use process, software needs specification, engineer training, etc.

Entity table   A list of entities from the domain of responsibility of the participants significant of a product or activity. This can be used as a template to help derive the necessary questions and metrics for a measurement programme.

ESPRIT   European Strategic Programme for Research and development in Information Technology. The **ami** project is part-funded by ESPRIT. The project has also used the research and experience from past ESPRIT projects, including REQUEST and MUSE.

Exploitation As in the exploitation of measurement data. Making decisions and then taking actions based on an analysis of the measurement data.

Goals A goal is an explicit formulation of what one is trying to achieve opposed to how one is going to act. The **ami** method contains two classes of goals, primary goals and sub-goals. Primary goals are high-level goals and sub-goals are derived from primary goals by analysis. Goals are also classified by their purpose – 'knowledge or resource' goals (monitoring, evaluation and prediction) and 'change or achievement' goals (increase, decrease and stabilize).

Goal-oriented measurement An approach for the application of metrics in industry that emphasizes the derivation of metrics from goals that are relevant to the specific needs of an organization. Similar terms are the global approach (since the first task in goal-oriented measurement is generally to characterize the process at a global level) or process-focused (since the emphasis on goals leads to an emphasis on what actions can be taken, i.e. improvement or changes in the work process). Goal-oriented measurement contrasts with model driven or data collection driven approaches.

GQM Goal/Question/Metric A framework for stating goals and refining them into specific questions about the characteristics that need to be measured. These questions provide a specification for the data needed to help address the goal. This framework was developed by V. Basili from the Software Engineering Laboratory at the University of Maryland when working in collaboration with the NASA Goddard Space Center. He has also applied it within various US companies. An adaptation of GQM has been incorporated into the **ami** method.

Goal tree A visual aid showing the primary goal at the top, and at lower levels, goals and sub-goals. A set of metrics is attached to the last level of sub-goals.

Initiator The main player in the programme is what we call the metrics initiator and is likely to be a senior manager with responsibility for sufficient budget to allocate a budget for use on a measurement programme. The metrics initiator is likely to have a number of projects under his or her control and will be responsible for the organization of the metrics programme although he or she may not necessarily be the person that does most of the actual work. The metrics initiator is likely to be the person who will justify the programme in business terms.

Maturity level A scale against which projects and organizations can be classified. The five maturity levels of the SEI Capability Maturity Model are: Initial, Repeatable, Defined, Managed and Optimized.

Measurement, to measure The activity of assigning numbers using a defined counting or evaluation process on the characteristics of a product or an activity.

Measurement data Values and identifiers that are given to characteristics, products or activities.

Measurement plan The way in which the activities of applying and using metrics is approached and applied in a particular working environment. Alternative terms are metrication plan, metrics programme, etc. Contrasts with informal measurement.

Measurement plan template Provided by the **ami** book to assist in the implementation of a metrics plan.

METKIT An ESPRIT project that produces training packages on software metrics. This is a useful complement to the **ami** book.

Metric A characteristic of a product or

process, e.g. delivered lines of code, project cost in man hours. A metric can be classified as objective or subjective depending on whether the data is the result of a counting process or subjective evaluation against a scale. Some metrics are computed from more primitive metrics, e.g. productivity. An alternative term for metric is a measure.

Metricate   Implementation of a measurement plan.

Metrics promoter   Reports to the metrics initiator and is responsible for the coordination and organization of the metrics initiative on a day-to-day basis. He or she is the person that is responsible for carrying out the planning and execution of the initiative.

Objective metric   See Metric.

Primitive metric   A new data item that is used to calculate a metric, e.g. timesheet bookings. A primitive metric is typically a metric that is not interpreted in isolation.

Process   An identified activity. The **ami** method is process-centred. People implement processes, which have resource inputs and product outputs. The focus is on the process because this is where decisions are made and this is where measurement data is needed for controlling and improving software development.

PYRAMID   The name of the ESPRIT project that promotes the use of metrics, but looks at measurement from case studies and the perspective of motivation for measurement.

SEI assessment procedure   A set of questions that can be used to define the maturity level of a project or organization. The Capability Maturity Model and assessment questions have been developed by the Software Engineering Institute at Carnegie Mellon University. (See also Capability Maturity Model.)

Software development   The activity of producing and maintaining software. It is composed of an organized process as well as mental processes (management, creative design work and knowledgeable use of technology).

Subjective metric   See Metric.

Index